EFFANBEE'S

Dy-Dee

THE COMPLETE COLLECTOR'S BOOK

EFFANBEE'S
Dy-Dee

THE COMPLETE COLLECTOR'S BOOK

BARBARA CRAIG HILLIKER

Reverie

PUBLISHING COMPANY

To purchase additional copies of this book, please contact:
Reverie Publishing Company
130 Wineow Street
Cumberland, Maryland 21502
888-721-4999

Library of Congress Control Number 2004090405

ISBN 1-932485-16-3

Project Editor: Krystyna Poray Goddu

Design: Arlene Lappen

Front and back cover photos: Robert M. Talbot

Cover photo: This 15-inch molded-hair Dy-Dee in near-mint condition
is from Mold 2. She has a hard-rubber head, a softer rubber body and flexible rubber ears.
She wears an original Effanbee cotton-lawn dress with green dots, which has buttons
and a buttonhole closure in the back and a deep hem. The dress also features a long sash
and white lace edging of high quality on the sleeves and collar, onto which
is stitched a tiny yellow silk ribbon bow.

Back cover photos: See pages 17, 52 and 94.

Printed and bound in Korea

DEDICATION

In memory of my mother, Isabel Stonex Craig,
and my grandmother, Jeff Reeves Stonex,
who gave me the baby dolls of my childhood.
For, Jack, my husband, who has brought joy to my life for 48 years,
and for our five beautiful real-live "babies":
Kate, Holly, Meg, Betsy and Steve.

Special thanks and appreciation to Peggy Montei
whose love for Dy-dee has made this book possible.
Her amazingly complete collection of Dy-Dee dolls, their layettes
and ephemera, forms the foundation of this book.

CONTENTS

FOREWORD · 8

INTRODUCTION · 13

CHAPTER ONE · 16
THE STORY OF THE EFFANBEE DOLL COMPANY

CHAPTER TWO · 22
THE DY-DEE DOLL

CHAPTER THREE · 52
DY-DEE'S LAYETTE

CHAPTER FOUR · 80
CASES, TRUNKS & FURNITURE

CHAPTER FIVE · 94
PUBLICATIONS & RELATED TOYS

CHAPTER SIX · 108
PUBLICITY & ADVERTISING

CHAPTER SEVEN · 116
OTHER DRINK-AND-WET DOLLS

CHAPTER EIGHT · 119
CLEANING & PRESERVING DY-DEE

CHAPTER NINE · 123
RE-CREATING THE DY-DEE BABY

CHAPTER TEN · 129
PATTERNS FOR AN 11-INCH DY-DEE LAYETTE

BIBLIOGRAPHY · 142

RESOURCES & CONTRIBUTORS · 144

This 13-inch baby is in wonderful condition for a Mold 1 doll. Her original box indicates she was made in the 1930s. She has high coloring and brunette molded hair; her eyes appear green, but were probably blue when she was made. She wears a long dusty-rose silk coat and bonnet, edged in ivory lace, by Effanbee over a white Effanbee christening gown.

FOREWORD

ACH GENERATION of women seems to remember one particular doll as the must-have toy of their childhood. For little girls born in the mid-1930s to 1950s, Effanbee's Dy-Dee Baby was such a doll. Many women who collect Dy-Dee dolls today never had one as a child. But for those who were fortunate enough to have had a Dy-Dee to play with, the memories seem to be especially vivid. In describing Dy-Dee, women find their senses re-engaged as they remember the wonderful "real" feeling of her skin, the sweet "baby smell" (probably the unique odor of virgin rubber used in the body) and the telltale squeak of rubber-on-rubber when Dy-Dee's legs or arms were moved. Some take on a look of wonder when describing how Dy-Dee could keep her eyes open, even when laid upon a flat surface, and yet could remain sleeping when held upright. This was a doll that engaged a child's imagination and affection as no doll had before. Whether a child had a

Dy-Dee of her very own, or could only play with a friend's doll, or read about Dy-Dee babies in a magazine, the attraction and mystique have lasted a lifetime. This "almost-human" baby doll seems to evoke a passionate and continuing response.

In 1943 I lived in Evansville, Indiana, across the street from a little girl, Kay Lynn Ziegler, who owned a 20-inch Dy-Dee. This doll soon became known as "Big Rubber" by all the potential little doll-mothers on the block. Some of the happiest hours of

These three Dy-Dee dolls, measuring 11 inches, 15 inches and 20 inches, are from Mold 2. The two larger dolls wear their Effanbee pink-and-white dresses, while the 11-inch example wears a white dimity dress with large flocked dots, also made by Effanbee.

The Dy-Dee that came "home" to Barbara Hilliker, fulfilling a childhood dream, is in her original layette box with a mixture of mama-made and Effanbee original clothing. The 11-inch doll from Mold 3 wears an original sun-suit, sweater and hat. The mittens are a later addition.

my childhood were spent caring for this remarkable doll, which belonged to this generous neighbor.

Years later, thumbing through a doll magazine, I saw a tiny picture of several dolls for sale. One that was barely visible was a Dy-Dee in her original trunk. I had long ago given up hope of ever finding a Dy-Dee to own. But here was a darling one, complete with layette and suitcase! With my heart pounding, I called the seller and could not believe my luck when I heard this baby was still available. Soon, the doll was on her way to me. The little Dy-Dee, in her wonderful pink Effanbee case filled with adorable layette items, renewed my childhood affection for this special doll, and started the chain of events that has culminated in the writing of this book.

Today, after almost seventy years, the amazing Dy-Dee babies still tug at the hearts of women who grew up yearning for this doll. What prompted such enduring affection? Part of the mystique of Dy-Dee may be a result of Effanbee's marketing strategy. Little girls were apparently eager to be told that having a Dy-Dee was a real responsibility because she needed lots of loving care. The need for all this extra care made Dy-Dee, the almost-human doll, very special to a generation of little girls. Many remember feeling that it was essential to "feed" Dy-Dee on a regular schedule, as well as seeing to her daily bath, walks and naps in the fresh air, along with frequent changes of clothing. As the mother of five children, grandmother of twelve, and great-grandmother of one, I believe I can trace the seeds of my own joy in motherhood to those happy hours spent caring for Dy-Dee baby.

One woman who has such a passion for these dolls that she is known today as "that Dy-Dee Baby Lady" also never owned a Dy-Dee as a child. However, Peggy Montei's mother instilled in her a love of dolls, coupled with a gentle spirit and an appreciation of how rich her childhood was, even though it did not include a Dy-Dee Baby! In 1939, when Peggy was four years old, she lived in the small town of St. Charles, Michigan. Her first memory of dolls is connected with a friend named Gracie O'Neill. She does not recall much about this friend, but she remembers her wonderful drink-and-wet doll very clearly!

The Christmas of 1940, Peggy received a Betsy-Wetsy doll. She still remembers the baby-powder scent, and can see all the beautiful pink-and-white clothing and accessories that came with the doll. She loved her new doll, and found it easy to pretend Betsy-Wetsy was a real baby. She would change her diaper and tuck her into her own little white basket. Peggy still owns that wicker basket.

The first rubber-bodied doll that Peggy saw as an adult was a Dy-Dee. Suddenly, those happy memories of childhood came back. She bought several Dy-Dee dolls in the following years, but did not begin to focus her collecting on the doll until 1993. Once she did, her challenge was to try to collect Dy-Dee furniture, cases, accessories and complete layettes appropriate for the different times in the life of Dy-Dee. Peggy found it very difficult

to discern which items were original to the dolls, and which had been lovingly added by a child. In seeking to correctly identify all the elements of Dy-Dee's world, Peggy discovered the excitement and satisfaction of research. In the past, Peggy had actually dreamed of a tiny baby, just doll-sized, that was alive and kicking her chubby legs. She believes that Dy-Dee dolls come as close as any doll to making her dream a reality.

In early 1993 I urged Patsy Moyer, publisher of the *Patsy & Friends Newsletter*, to devote one issue to Dy-Dee dolls. Patsy did not think her readers would be very interested, but she announced that she would try to collect enough material for an article in the newsletter. She soon had enough responses and photographs to devote two entire issues of the newsletter to Dy-Dee dolls.

It was in the pages of this excellent publication that Peggy and I first met. This long-awaited book began with a question Peggy sent to the *Patsy and*

Peggy Montei, dedicated Dy-Dee collector and historian, holds a small mystery Dy-Dee from Mold 1 with a red-blonde caracul wig, wearing an original dress, nightingale and Effanbee oil-cloth shoes. Wigs were not commonly used on the dolls until long after this one was produced, and only two wigged early Mold 1 examples have been found. But as this head is not painted under the wig, we must assume the wig was put on at the factory. (Photo courtesy of Lynn Schriber)

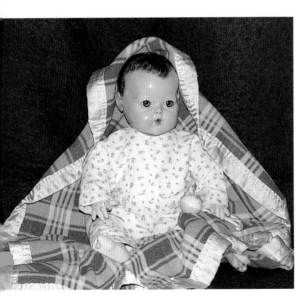

One of Peggy Montei's favorite Dy-Dees is this 20-inch baby in its original blue-flowered white flannel pajamas. The baby is kept cozy in a soft blue-and-white plaid blanket that wrapped Peggy's brother when he was a baby.

The Dy-Dee babies came in several sizes. Even dolls from the same mold may look quite different, as these "sisters" from Mold 1 demonstrate. The 15-inch and 11-inch Dy-Dees are wearing their matching organdy dresses, complete with pretty ruffled bonnets and pompom-tied booties.

Nearly life-size, this 20-inch Dy-Dee from Mold 2 is all ready for a buggy ride in her vintage wicker carriage. She wears her original pink-and-white Effanbee layette sweater and cap.

Friends Newsletter in late 1993. In it she wished that "someone would publish a book on Dy-Dee; there are so many different faces, plus all the clothing, cases, furniture and accessories." Shortly thereafter, Peggy journeyed to Chicago and the United Federation of Doll Clubs (UFDC) National Convention so that the two ladies who shared such a passion for Dy-Dee dolls could meet. A warm friendship formed in the next years as we

corresponded and shared information about Dy-Dee. In 2002 I asked Peggy if she thought the timing was right for a book devoted to Dy-Dee dolls. She did, and using her carefully selected and extensive collection of Dy-Dee dolls as the foundation, I began to work on this book.

Peggy's mother instilled in her a life-long love of dolls, as well as sharing her love of reading and writing, and she credits her mother with the inspiration and encouragement that allowed her to dream of a book about Dy-Dee dolls. Her dream, and that of Dy-Dee lovers everywhere, has become a reality with this book.

The study of the Dy-Dee baby is multi-faceted. For individuals who enjoy a rags-to-riches story, there is the history of the Effanbee Doll Company and its two founders, who brought great innovation and integrity to doll manufacturing. For those interested in successful marketing schemes, there is much to be learned from the practices of this doll company, which thrived at a time when the nation was slowly recovering from the Great Depression. There remains today an appreciation for the creative business acumen of Bernard Fleischaker and Hugo Baum, who found new ways to promote their dolls and create a vital market for them. And then, far removed from the business of dolls, there is the engaging history of three decades of little girls who fell in love with this chubby infant, whose many charming ways seemed to blur the line between dolls and real babies.

INTRODUCTION

T HE HISTORY of the Effanbee Doll Company and that of the Dy-Dee baby doll are bound to-gether in one of the best examples of an American success story in the world of doll manufacturing. The trust and warm friendship between the two founders, Bernard E. Fleischaker and Hugo Baum, seems to have set their company apart from other dollmaking firms. From the beginning in 1910, they sought to offer products of high quality and to create a retail market in which parents were willing to spend money to buy the best dolls for their daughters. Fleischaker and Baum may have been among the first to realize that there was a market for mass-produced dolls of high quality. The Dy-Dee baby ultimately made use of all the lessons Fleischaker and Baum had learned up to the year of its introduction in 1933. Dy-Dee was an instant success and a long-standing sales leader for this company, which used the motto "Finest and Best" to describe

7625

HONEY GIRL — Lovely little Lucinda steps right out of the pages of a book, skates and all. She has loads of charm in her lacy, frilly old-fashioned costume, her peaches-and-cream complexion, her pretty blond hair. Available in 14", 16" and 18" sizes.

EFFANBEE means "Finest and Best"

When you buy a doll for a little girl, only the best is good enough—because *her doll* is one of the most important things in her life. It's heartbreaking for a child to fasten her affection on a doll that doesn't last. That's why *EFFANBEE* makes only the best dolls. You can spend much or little for an *EFFANBEE* doll but whichever you buy you can be sure it will last and be loved for a long, long while. Look for the golden *EFFANBEE* heart—it's your guarantee of quality.

their approach to making dolls.

From its inception, the success of the Effanbee Doll Company was due in large part to the innovative marketing approach used by Fleischaker and Baum. One ex-ample of this business acumen was their decision to include six black-and-white photographs of Bubbles, a large baby doll, with each doll sold. In an advertisement in the Montgomery Ward catalog of 1926 the child mother was encouraged to send the photographs of her new baby to her

Effanbee found many ways to keep their name and motto— "Finest and Best"— in front of the public. Every accessory, packaged outfit and doll they sold included an Effanbee leaflet.

grandmother, aunts and other relatives.

Other innovations used by Effanbee to increase doll sales included a 1929 advertising campaign based upon an offer to send a golden-colored metal Effanbee heart necklace in exchange for a magazine coupon and six cents. In another successful campaign, in 1930, the company gave away a choice of three dolls in exchange for three subscriptions to a magazine. Perhaps their most original and effective approach to selling dolls was the publication of *The Patsytown News*. Initially, Effanbee sent this newsletter to stores that sold their dolls. Soon, Effanbee was "helping" Aunt Patsy mail copies of the newsletter out to members of the Patsy Doll Club. Effanbee mailed 250,000 copies to club members four times a year.

In order to better understand the phenomenon of Dy-Dee's success, it is helpful to examine the social history immediately preceding the doll's introduction. A significant shift in the production of dolls and toys occurred at the time of World War I (1914-1918). Prior to this period, France and Germany were the recognized leaders in the manufacture of dolls. When all imports from France and Germany ceased during the war, the doll and toy industry turned to America and Japan as the new leaders in production of these items. Effanbee was ready for this leadership role and introduced new dolls rapidly. By 1918 they offered one hundred fifty different dolls in more than three hundred styles. In 1918 Effanbee proudly introduced their new motto: "American Dolls are now the World's Standard."

One reason for the success of the Dy-Dee Baby may stem, in part, from an article written by Dr. Walter Hough and published in *The New York Times* in 1927. The text was originally presented at the American Association for the Advancement of Science, during the eighty-third annual meeting. In his article Dr. Hough wrote that dolls are not associated with lower levels of culture, and that elegant dolls made for the doll shops of Paris by such illustrious names as Jumeau and Bru were too perfect to be sought out and loved by children. This concept is supported by other articles that have noted that many children were "afraid of their huge Sunday dolls"—for fear the

Advertisements for Dy-Dee Baby, like this example from 1941, were carefully styled to give little girls and their parents the idea that this doll would bring hours of happy play value. Of course, the qualities that make Dy-Dee so unique were also highlighted.

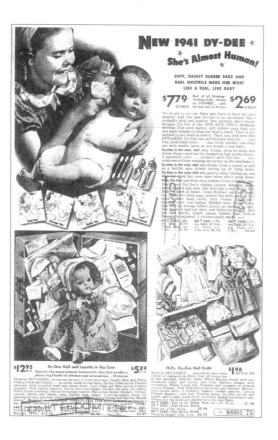

dolls would tip over and hurt them!

Dr. Hough wrote: "The place and significance of the doll in modern (1927) life are of great importance. No one can fully realize the profound and beneficial effects of the doll on the plastic child, or adequately reckon the value of the combination of play and education." Dr. Hough was expressing the new concept that children were "plastic"—that is to say, malleable, and that the adults they would become would grow out of the lessons learned in childhood, at school and at play.

The evolution of realistic baby dolls and the emphasis on play value of toys began in 1903-1904, when the psychology of childhood and the need for play were first closely examined. The movement towards dolls that looked like real babies and children began in Germany. Marion Kaulitz is credited with beginning this revolution when she designed dolls that were then modeled by Paul Vogelsanger, and displayed by Hermann Tietz in 1909. These dolls, known as the Munich Art Dolls, were destined to usher in the new approach to realistic dollmaking in Europe and the United States.

The natural result of making dolls that looked like real children was to create a new emphasis on the proper way to care for a doll. Effanbee understood this necessity very well. They consciously created dolls that could elicit love and affection from their owners. At this time, psychologists were suggesting that doll play was the best way to nurture a girl's dormant maternal instinct. They surmised that unless this maternal instinct was awakened in childhood, girls would grow up to seek "companionate marriages and become one-child mothers."

The stage was set for a warm acceptance of the realistic dolls of high quality that Effanbee was ready to introduce. The ultimate doll, in terms of the desirable new realism, was the Dy-Dee baby—a doll that not only looked like a real baby, but also acted like one: drinking her bottle, wetting her diaper and requiring hours of mothering from her child mother.

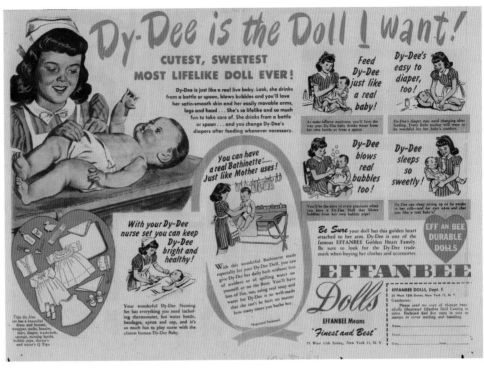

Opportunities for creative play through Dy-Dee were marketed in magazines, newspapers and the Effanbee's own publications. This colorful ad from the Sunday comics ran in October 1947.

CHAPTER ONE

THE STORY OF THE EFFANBEE DOLL COMPANY

ERNARD E. FLEISCHAKER AND HUGO BAUM met when each operated his own small business in Atlantic City, New Jersey. Fleischaker sold furniture while Baum sold shopping bags. Baum, a native of the toy-making region of Thuringia in Germany, had moved to the United States only twelve years before meeting his friend, Bernard Fleischaker, who was born in Kentucky. The men formed their own company of Fleischaker and Baum in 1910 in New York City. They named their company "Eff-ann-Bee," using the first initials of their last names. The name was later simplified by dropping the hyphens and one of the "n"s.

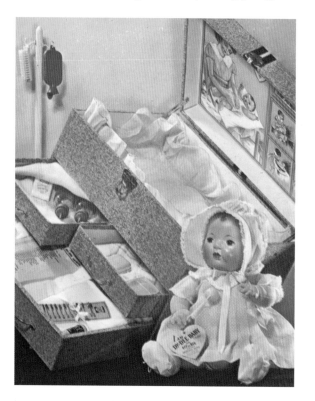

A publicity photo from late 1930 presented Dy-Dee in her elaborate layette case, filled with wonderful clothing and accessories. Note the lovely pillow-mattress edged with deep organdy ruffles. The doll is a Dy-Dee-ette, 11 inches, Mold 1. (Courtesy *Fortune* magazine)

Initially, they were primarily toy "jobbers," purchasing toys from manufacturers and then selling them to retail merchants. By 1912 the two men felt they had learned enough to begin the manufacture of their own doll designs. At first, they imported molds from Germany, then had Frederick Devoll in Providence, Rhode Island, make the heads. These first dolls were somewhat lacking in finesse and style, and were referred to as "being made of concrete-type composition." But by 1912 Effanbee had imported a mold from Gebruder Heubach, and the resulting doll was offered as a premium for sending one subscription plus eighty-five cents to the *The People's Home Journal*. From the earliest days, the Effanbee marketing approach led to Hugo Baum being known as the

Three Dy-Dee sisters are ready for a bedtime story in their pajamas with the pink-and-blue Dy-Dee logo. The big sister with the caracul wig is 15 inches, with a Mold 2 head. On the right is a 9-inch Dy-Dee-Wee from Mold 1. Her pajamas have no feet, and tie in the back at the neck. On the left is an 11-inch Dy-Dee from Mold 3, wearing the classic footed sleeper with a faux waistband and button closure in back.

The process of dollmaking has always been labor-intensive. The manufacture of Dy-Dee dolls involved time-consuming hands-on labor. Whether the end result is to be hard or soft rubber, the initial process is the same. (Courtesy *Fortune* magazine)

"Ziegfield of the doll industry," a title he thoroughly enjoyed.

As their dollmaking skills increased, Fleischaker and Baum's business improved as well. They began engaging in interstate commerce in 1914. During 1918, "Effanbee" became a registered trademark with the United States Patent Office. In 1919, as World War I was ending, Effanbee placed a full-page advertisement in *Playthings*, a magazine for the toy trade, to emphasize the fact that their products were all "made in America." The two friends took great pride in the fact they were manufacturing American-made dolls for American children.

Hugo Baum was part of Effanbee until his death in 1940. After his death, Fleischaker left the company the two friends had formed, and moved to California where he formed a new company called Fleischaker Novelties. Hugo Baum's son, Bernard, took over the reins of Effanbee. Bernard Fleischaker's brother, Walter, remained as one of Effanbee's top salesmen until his retirement in 1945.

Another man who helped shape Dy-Dee and Effanbee's successful sale of the doll was Al Kirchof. He was a significant part of Effanbee from 1930 to 1980, when he retired. He had the rather thankless task of trying to sell dolls to stores during the Great Depression of the 1930s. Late in his career, his advice on which dolls to buy was eagerly sought by store buyers, who had come to trust his feeling for the doll market.

At a time when labor unions were active in ninety percent of the dollmaking companies in New York City, Effanbee was the only major producer in New York City to fight them off. The labor unions were able to improve wages and working conditions from the sweatshop practices common in dollmaking companies prior to unionization. The unions were responsible for four toy-making companies fleeing the city. This ultimately re-sulted in an agreement between the union and the doll manu-facturers that no dollmaker who signed could move outside the city. Effanbee was apparently able to retain its work force with-out union interference because the company paid fair wages and offered improved working conditions. The continuity of the workforce helped Effanbee realize its goal of making dolls of fine quality for American children in America.

Effanbee also benefited from the talents of master artisan Bernard Lipfert, sculptor extraordinaire of beautiful baby doll heads. Lipfert had served his apprenticeship in pre-war Germany, in Thuringia, the fourth generation of his family to train as a toy maker. When he moved to Brooklyn, New York, in 1912, he be-came a free-lance "doll modeler." In an article in the December 1936 issue of *Fortune* magazine, he was quick to point out he did not consider himself a sculptor; insisting instead that "doll mod-eling is an art of its own with rules of its own." Lipfert charged from fifty dollars to five hundred dollars to model a head. He frequently tweaked his own designs to create similar models for rival dollmaking companies. Interestingly, the same article in *Fortune* chose to attempt to define what a doll is and is not, a dis-cussion that continues today among doll artists. Dollmakers seemed to agree in 1936 "that a doll is something to be played with, by girls up to twelve and little boys under six." Further, they agreed that a doll cannot be a "flossy lamp shade or a boudoir pillow or a pincushion. It cannot be an arty figurine, the sort that appeals mainly to adults. It can not be a dime-store gimcrack that floats in a baby's bath or goes soggy in baby's mouth—the (doll) trade views the bulk of these as 'novelties'."

Bernard Lipfert noted in the article that "the art of modeling dolls is not quite the art of sculpture. A sculptor strives for a faithful likeness; but a doll that looked exactly like a baby would be a commercial flop. In a doll's face, the roundness of the cheeks, upturn of the nose, wideness of the eyes are accentuat-ed; the mouth is shrunk to a rosebud." Before Lipfert began modeling doll heads, most of the heads were characterized by a "universally dumb expression." Put another way, Lipfert said he

To harden rubber, the heads are steam-cured at 300 degrees. In this photo, the molds are being broken open to remove the still-soft rubber heads. (Courtesy *Fortune* magazine)

Bernard Lipfert, an independent doll modeler working in Brooklyn, New York, was the "father" of Dy-Dee Baby and many other beloved baby doll faces. (Courtesy *Fortune* magazine)

had the "talent of modeling heads that achieve the effect of a lifelike little doll, without going so far as to suggest a doll-like little girl."

Although Dy-Dee may be one of the most famous of the Effanbee baby dolls, she was not the first baby this creative pair introduced. Their first real success came with the introduction of Baby Dainty, a composition shoulder-head doll with a cloth body in 1912. Baby Dainty continued to be part of Effanbee's line until 1926. In 1913 she was offered with a pacifier, even though she was made with a closed mouth. This is the first example of the depth of understanding Fleischaker and Baum had for their customers' needs. They seem to have realized from the beginning that little girls wanted their dolls to be as "real" as possible. They also discovered that baby and toddler dolls in short dresses outsold their long-dress costumed contemporaries. Effanbee offered a variety of mama dolls, advertised as being able to "walk, talk, and sleep"—even when the doll could not do any of these things!

In January 1926 the next Effanbee baby to make a big impression was introduced in *Playthings*. Bubbles, a baby doll with a very happy face, sold from 1926 to 1931. She had a bent arm to allow the doll to "suck" on her finger. This baby's head was taken from the head mold for a popular German porcelain doll, Baby Gloria, then re-sculpted by Lipfert to have a deeply dimpled face, painted or sleep eyes, very chubby baby arms and legs made of composition, like the head, and a cuddly cloth body.

Always an innovator, Effanbee was the first to offer black dolls nationally in 1915. In 1927 Effanbee introduced the first American doll that looked like an actual child: the now famous and beloved Patsy doll, and one of Lipfert's early successes. Patsy was soon joined by a whole family of additional dolls—all of which were widely copied in the doll industry. Perhaps more importantly, Patsy added a whole new element to the business of selling dolls: the specially made doll wardrobe. Effanbee picked up this concept and began executing it quickly and well, enhancing future dolls in their line with increasingly elaborate wardrobes and the trunks to hold them.

Shortly thereafter, in 1934, Effanbee introduced Dy-Dee, the first baby doll that could drink from a bottle or spoon and, after a time-delay, wet its diapers, just like a real baby. After modeling the head for the Dy-Dee baby in 1933, Lipfert tried to talk Effanbee out of using it. He considered it the "dumbest head I ever saw." But Hugo Baum knew his market and felt the time was right for his next innovation. Dy-Dee did indeed become the next happy success story for Effanbee.

In 1946 Noma Electric Company purchased Effanbee Doll Company, which they owned until 1953. During that time, the quality of Effanbee dolls began to slip. Bernard Baum, along with associates Morris Lutz and Perry Epstein, then took over management of Effanbee until it was sold in 1971 to Leroy Fadem, who became chairman of the board, and Roy R. Raizen, who became president.

In 1987 the Russ-Berrie company purchased Effanbee. Five years later, in 1992, the Alexander Doll Company became its new owner and turned its operations over to Stanley and Irene Wahlberg who, with Margiann Flanagan, purchased it from Alexander in 1995. In 2002 the Tonner Doll Company, owned by Robert Tonner, acquired the Effanbee Doll Company. Tonner, a noted doll artist and manufacturer, immediately began working to restore the company's reputation for fabrics and designs of fine quality, both for the dolls and the accessories.

Under Robert Tonner's direction, Effanbee reissued several of the Patsy family dolls in 2003, dressing them in clothing reproduced from the original outfits. Brenda Starr Reporter was also re-issued as a beautiful fashion doll. In 2004 Effanbee is reissuing the Dy-Dee Baby in the 11-inch size, complete with a marvelous layette based on the original wardrobes. (See chapter nine for the complete story of the recreation of Dy-Dee.)

The wonderful face that Bernard Lipfert sculpted is now well known and beloved as the first Dy-Dee Baby. This 20-inch doll is the largest of the Mold 1 dolls.

CHAPTER TWO

THE DY-DEE DOLL

T HE GROUNDWORK FOR DY-DEE began in 1931-32. At that time, dolls with rubber limbs and cloth bodies were being offered by Effanbee and by Ideal. In 1933, with the creation of Dy-Dee, Effanbee brought its dream of an all-rubber baby doll to fruition. In 1934 Effanbee began advertising Dy-Dee as their newest and most amazing doll. In order to understand the success of Dy-Dee, it is best to examine the doll and her development over a number of years.

This bright-eyed 15-inch Dy-Dee from Mold 1 wears an Effanbee dress and bonnet.

From the very beginning, Dy-Dee was designed to be a doll of high quality. Careful attention was paid to every detail of her face, body and beautiful layette. The first Dy-Dee doll has a heavy hard-rubber head, with a body made of softer, high-grade, virgin rubber. Bernard Lipfert modeled her realistic face to have rounded pink baby cheeks and an open mouth that shows off her molded tongue. The lips are painted a vivid red. The body is beautifully sculpted, with all the baby-fat wrinkles one would expect to see in a small infant. Her hands feature separated fingers, with the middle two fingers positioned slightly below the others. Her fat feet have clearly defined toes with dimples and a lifted big toe. Even her little navel is carefully sculpted with a roll of fat above it. The first Dy-Dee has molded hair that appears to be softly curled, just like the hair of real babies. The hair is painted a shade of brunette—the hue varies on different dolls from light brown to a very dark brown.

This 15-inch baby from Mold 3 wears a yellow "eiderdown" snow-suit with matching bonnet. Both are trimmed in blue braid. The snow-suit may be original, but this is the first time we have seen it in yellow. The doll has green eyes and very nice coloring.

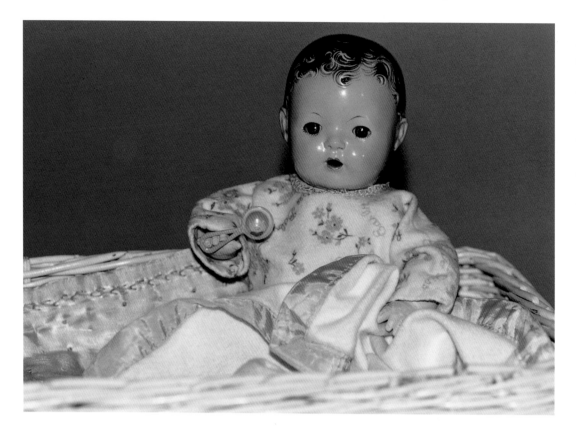

The hard-rubber heads of the Mold I Dy-Dee dolls have great detail. Notice the clearly defined curls and life-like ears on this 9-inch Dy-Dee-Wee. She is wearing Dy-Dee Logo pajamas with a pink-and-blue print and she holds a Dy-Dee rattle from her layette.

The extra-hard finish on the hard-rubber Dy-Dee heads gives a very high sheen to the surface of the face. This 11-inch Dy-Dee-ette wears a silk-taffeta pink full-length coat, made with a short capelet over the shoulders, along with her original bonnet and long white dress.

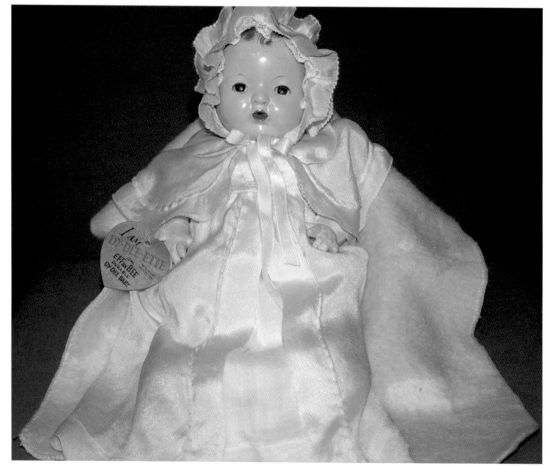

Effanbee gave this new baby lovely sleep-eyes made of celluloid. Within two years, some of the eyes were changed to tin, and later to glassine. She also has upper eyelashes of real hair, and deftly painted lower lashes. The heads of the early dolls have beautifully detailed curls, as well as dainty little ears. The first head mold, often referred to as Mold 1, bears all these features.

In 1940 Effanbee announced their newest innovation: Dy-Dee dolls now came with attached, flexible rubber ears. In addition, caracul skin wigs were available on some dolls. Later, Effanbee redefined Dy-Dee's little up-turned nose and open her nostrils. In the 1950s Dy-Dee was given two tiny holes below her eyes so that she could weep "real tears." Every effort was made throughout Dy-Dee's production to create the most life-like doll possible.

The Dy-Dee heads from Mold 1 have clearly defined features—much like the precise detail that is achieved in the first few pours of a porcelain doll head mold. The rubber of the head is so smoothly finished that to those doll collectors who have not studied Dy-Dee closely it may look like composition or hard plastic. But if one of these dolls is dropped, the head can shatter—even though Effanbee advertised Dy-Dee as an "unbreakable" doll. The fragility of the head is a result of the process used in finishing the rubber on these heads. The hard rubber head also gives the doll a substantial lifelike feeling and heft when she is held. During the finishing process, the painting on the hard rubber heads was sealed and thus looks fresh for years. The original finish of these Mold 1 dolls has a high sheen.

The Mold 1 face is distinct from the other Dy-Dee faces, as

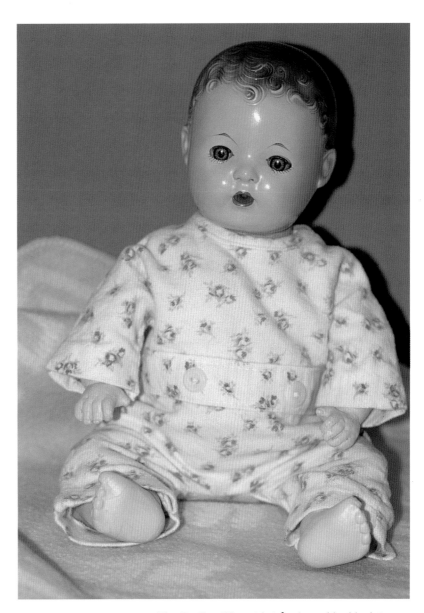

This Dy-Dee-Wee with a fresh-scrubbed look is wearing original pajamas with a faux waistband and two-button trim. She is sitting on a bunny blanket made by the Esmond Mills in New England.

This 15-inch Dy-Dee from Mold 1 has a very red open mouth with molded tongue that just fits the nipple of the Dy-Dee nursing bottle.

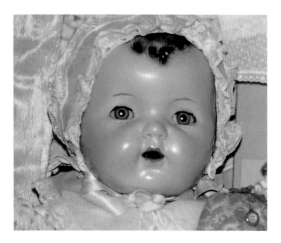

Although the mouth of this 20-inch doll is painted in the same manner as the 15-inch doll above, it appears to be less widely opened.

As Dy-Dee's size changes, so does the look of her features. The 11-inch Dy-Dee-ette has yet another look to her bright-red open mouth.

well as from other dolls of her time. The eyes are set wide and low in the face to resemble a newborn baby. Her little nose and wide mouth are placed close to the center of the face, augmenting the newborn-baby look. The mouth is open as though she were singing "Ahhhh." The faces of later Dy-Dees have pert little rosebud mouths shaped as though the doll were singing "Oh."

Except for the very earliest dolls, Dy-Dees are clearly marked. A variety of identifying words and numbers are embossed on the body and/or the head. The first Dy-Dee dolls do not even bear the Effanbee name. However, the Mold 1 face is unique enough to be easy to recognize. The first heads have tiny numbers embossed on the lower neck. One can surmise the numbers were used in sequential order, but no mention of these numbers was made in Effanbee records. Numbers that have been verified on the 15-inch Mold 1 dolls include: 1, 3, 4, 5, 6, 10, 11 and 12. The exception to this numbering are the heads from Mold 1 with painted blonde hair; these dolls have no marks whatsoever on the head. When Effanbee began putting their company name and patent numbers on the dolls' upper backs, the first such identifying information was

Amazingly, the early Dy-Dee dolls, which are marked only with a stamp on their rubber bodies, have retained their markings for nearly seventy years.

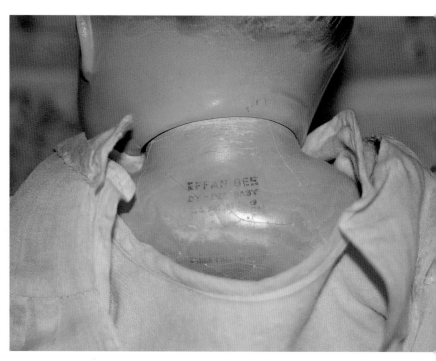

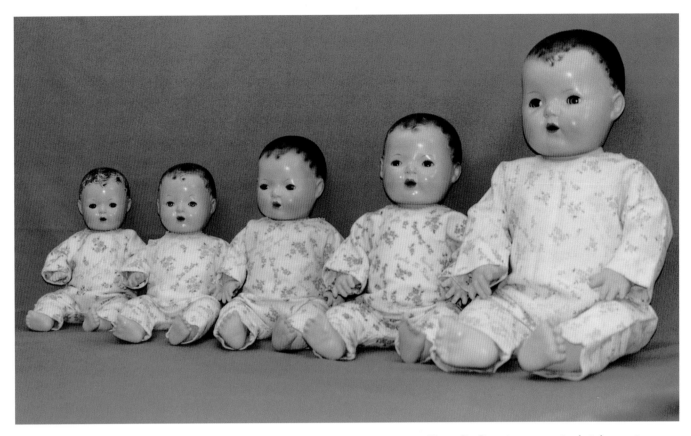

These Dy-Dee sisters pose in their logo pajamas for a family portrait. This picture offers a good opportunity to study how Dy-Dee heads from the same mold number appear to change as the size is reduced. There is a strong family resemblance, but the dolls also display definite differences.

stamped in black ink directly on the upper back of the doll, just below the neck. Soon the company name and patent numbers were made as part of the mold, so each doll came with embossed identification on the rubber body and head. The Dy-Dee bodies remained marked throughout its production, but the heads are not consistently marked.

All the rubber parts for Dy-Dee were made by Miller Rubber Co. Inc. in Akron, Ohio. When Dy-Dee became a runaway success, this company brought out their own version of a drink-and-wet doll, featuring a hard rubber head made with a substance called Millite. This doll never approached the popularity of Dy-Dee.

The first Dy-Dee doll was 15 inches in length, but additional sizes were soon added. Dolls with Mold 1 heads were available in three sizes: 11 inches, 14 inches and a nearly life-size 20 inches. The prices ranged from $2.89 to $7.98. Eventually, Dy-Dee was also available in a 9-inch size and a 13-inch size.

Of special interest to collectors is an article in *The Patsytown News*, Volume 2, Number 2, published in 1935, which announces

The first member of the Dy-Dee family is 15 inches tall and her name is simply Dy-Dee. Her round little face has the look of a very young baby. Her eyes have a definite almond shape. Her painted hair is usually brown, but is occasionally found with a lighter blonde color. Dy-Dee originally had blue or brown sleep-eyes but, due to the aging process, these dolls' eyes often look green or hazel when found today.

the arrival of Dy-Dee's baby sister, 11-inch Dy-Dee-ette. The new baby was also featured in an advertisement in *Playthings,* in the June 1936 issue. The Dy-Dee family now included four dolls whose names denoted their size: Dy-Dee-ette, 11 inches; Dy-Dee-Kin, 13 inches; Dy-Dee, 15 inches; and Dy-Dee Lou, 20 inches.

In 1937, the Dy-Dee Family grew again when the 9-inch Dy-Dee-Wee was featured in Effanbee advertising. The tiniest of the Dy-Dee family, this doll is highly prized by collectors today. This small version was offered with all the same layette items and trunks as her larger sisters. But she appears to have had a very brief production history; hence, these precious little ones are the most difficult of the Dy-Dee babies to find today.

In addition to the above-mentioned names, Dy-Dee was also advertised under the following names: Dy-Dee Ellen, 11 inches; Dy-Dee Jane, 15 inches; Dy-Dee Lu, 20 inches. Even the spelling of Dy-Dee's name was not consistent. Effanbee seems to have always preferred to spell Dy-Dee's name with a hyphen, but the hyphen is sometimes missing in commercial catalogs and advertising. Sometimes the second "D" is capitalized; sometimes it is not.

In order to recognize the different faces that were used for Dy-Dee, a careful examination of their features is required. The differences between dolls from Mold 1 and Mold 2 are obvious enough that these two are usually identified correctly. However, the differences between Mold 2 and Mold 3 are much more

A close-up of the Mold 1 head shows the detail of her distinctly molded curls. The hair color is softly painted to enhance the sense of a very young baby.

subtle, especially on the 15-inch dolls. Therefore, they are the most difficult to identify with confidence. The following comparison, in pictures and words, is meant as a guide for those who wish to identify the mold number of their dolls.

The first doll, named simply Dy-Dee, is 15 inches and has a wonderful face and body. Her almond-shaped eyes are spaced widely apart and are rather small relative to the size of her head. The earliest eyes appear to have been celluloid, with later ones being made of tin. Eventually, the eyes were made of glassine. The eyes could be blue or brown, which may have aged to a green or hazel today. This Dy-Dee has painted lower lashes and upper lashes of human-hair or mohair or, later, a synthetic material. Her mouth is very red and open, showing her tongue molded to hold the nipple of her bottle perfectly. Her eyebrows are deep brown and arched, made with a single stroke of a paint brush.

The nose is rather wide and there is only a minimal indention at the bridge of the nose. The nostrils are shallow and have a single red dot in each one. If you look at this Dy-Dee head in profile, the forehead has a minimal slope down to the nose, and the end of the nose is rounded and blunt, not pert and turned up. In other words, when you look at this doll's profile, the eyes are set back from the bridge of the nose, which is gently curved. Her cheeks are pink and the overall finish to her head is very smooth and firm. The hair is beautifully detailed, with a telltale curl on the middle of the forehead. The suggestion of soft baby curls surrounding her face, ears and neck is carved into the head mold. The hands are very pudgy in appearance, with the fingers well separated. The toes on her fat little feet are also separately

Trunks filled with adorable layette clothing and properly sized accessories were available even for the tiniest 9-inch Dy-Dee-Wee babies.

The unique "spoon" hands on these two 9-inch babies help identify the Dy-Dee-Wee, even from a photograph. All the larger Dy-Dee dolls have fingers that are spread further apart.

defined. On the back of this doll's head, on the lower neck, the number 10 is inscribed. Embossed on the rubber back, between the shoulder blades, is the word EFF-AN-BEE, below which is the name: DY-DEE BABY. A series of patent numbers is below the name. An earlier version of this same doll has the number 5 on the back of her neck, but there are no marks on her body. The earliest Dy-Dee dolls in the worst condition seem to have the lowest numbers, according to Peggy Montei. The written records of the early Effanbee Company are lost, but we may surmise that the numbers relate to different productions of the heads, as they do not seem to relate to the size of the head.

The 9-inch Dy-Dee is marked on the back lower neck of her head: EFF-AN-BEE DY-DEE. The rubber body is also marked with the Effanbee name. The fingers on the hands are formed together, with no separation. This style of hand is sometimes called a "spoon hand" by collectors. The big toes on her tiny feet are slightly separated from the other toes. The head on the 9-inch babies features very deeply carved, molded curls. The mouth is open, but does not appear to have a tongue. The sleep eyes have human-hair, mohair or synthetic lashes on the upper eye lids and delicately painted lower lashes. I have two in my collection, both marked with the number 24 just below the words on her lower neck. Other numbers that have been verified for the 9-inch Dy-Dee are 5, 15, 20 and 31. Their significance remains a mystery. The fingers on the small hands are not separated. This smallest Dy-Dee was made from Mold 1.

The Mold 1 Dy-Dee dolls are usually found with brunette hair. The detail of soft curls, which is in the mold, is quite distinct. Notice the definite curl in the center of the forehead.

If you look at her hands straight-on, it is easy to see the all-together fingers on the 9-inch Dy-Dee's hands.

Although the closed fingers on the 9-inch Dy-Dee look fairly flat when viewed from above, as in photo on page 31, when viewed from the palm side, a slight bending inwards of the fingers is visible.

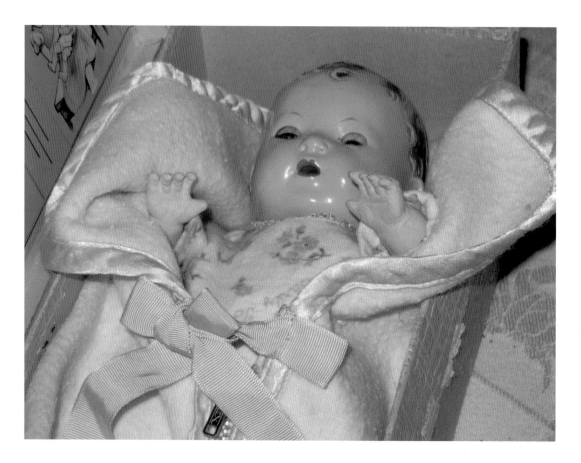

These three Dy-Dee dolls are wearing the familiar pink-and-white clothing sold by Effanbee. The three examples have dark-brown painted hair and are 11, 15, and 20 inches tall.

The 20-inch Dy-Dee dolls from Mold 3 are easy to recognize, but the 15 and 11 inch sizes are more difficult to identify. This trio of Mold 3 dolls in various sizes all wear Dy-Dee clothing made by Effanbee.

It is worth noting that Effanbee was obviously aware that there was a market for rubber baby dolls that were less costly than Dy-Dee. In 1936 the Montgomery Ward catalog featured a rubber baby doll on one corner of the cover, made by Effanbee, but not a Dy-Dee. This baby was 10½ inches long, could drink her bottle and then wet her diaper. She came with her own nursing bottle, wearing only a diaper—all for just 69 cents! Obviously, Effanbee was eager to provide dolls to many little girls—whatever their economic level might be.

Doll collectors know that when molds for heads are shrunk, the resulting smaller heads may have only a passing "family resemblance" to the larger versions of the same doll. Careful examination of the details of each doll is necessary to make an accurate identification. Further complicating the identification of Dy-Dee dolls, some of the babies have caracul wigs, others have painted molded hair, and some that have lost their wigs have hair that was painted on by early owners. In ads in 1937, brunette is the only color listed for Dy-Dee's hair. But charming versions of Dy-Dee with the Mold 1 head have also been found with blonde painted hair. The second and third mold dolls

With a pink bow in her hair and a vintage mother-made cotton dress, this 15-inch Dy-Dee from Mold 2 is ready for a romp with her sturdy wooden pull-toy. Hand-knit booties complete her ensemble.

Many collectors are particularly drawn to the rare Dy-Dee babies with blonde hair. This example is one of the original 15-inch dolls and she wears her all-original long pink silk coat and bonnet and her dainty christening gown.

have less clearly defined carved hair. Also, the Mold 2 doll's hair is often painted in a heavy-handed manner, which makes it appear as a solid block, rather than having the delicate feathered look of the hair on the Mold 1 Dy-Dees.

The second mold for Dy-Dee is one of the most beloved. This may be, in part, because it was the first edition of Dy-Dee to have the amazing, flexible rubber ears. The eyes on dolls from Mold 2 are very round and larger than on those from the first mold. The eyebrow is now a faint single paint stroke in a shallow arch. The doll has upper eyelashes of hair and long painted lower lashes. The lower lashes on the Mold 1 dolls are short and barely curved to the side, while the lashes on the Mold 2 dolls have a decided curve to the outside corner of each eye. The mouth is small and opens more vertically than the Mold 1 dolls' mouths. There is only the faintest suggestion of a tongue. The profile of this baby's head shows a much deeper indentation between the eyes, at the bridge of the nose. The molded hair no longer looks curly. It has waves just

This Dy-Dee from Mold 2 shows the somewhat "clumpy" look of the hair painting found in many dolls from Mold 2. She is wearing her original organdy bonnet with a hem-stitched deep ruffle.

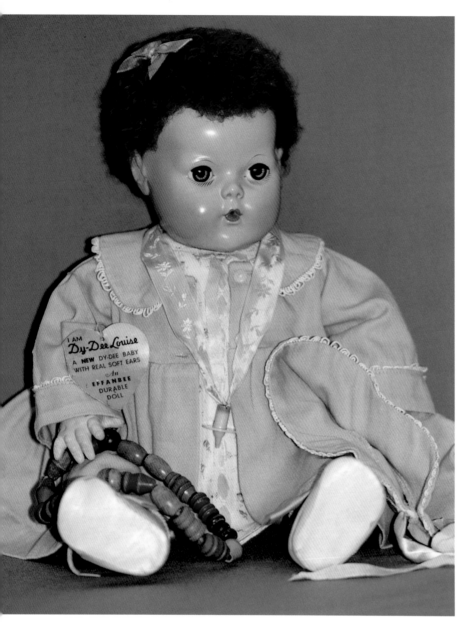

Lovely Dy-Dee Louise, a 20-inch baby from Mold 2, has dark-auburn caracul hair. She wears her blue Effanbee coat over her original white-with-blue design dimity dress. She has a bow in her hair, her pacifier around her neck on a silk ribbon, and her original oil-cloth shoes. Her matching blue hat is by her side.

barely suggested by detailing in the mold. The big toes on the doll's feet are now definitely separated and turned up towards the legs. While there are no markings on the head, embossed on the upper back is the company name, in very small letters, and the doll's name in quite large letters, as well as the patent numbers. These dolls were offered with caracul wigs as well as with molded hair.

The caracul wigs used for Dy-Dee are of the finest quality. They could be shampooed repeatedly, then combed and brushed to a soft fluff. The most common color for Dy-Dee's hair, whether it is painted or a skin wig, is brunette. There were blonde babies as well, but these are relatively rare. Some Dy-Dee dolls have a decidedly red cast to their hair.

The faces of the Mold 3 dolls are very similar to those of Mold 2, but there are subtle differences. Perhaps the easiest place to see this is the rather puffy-looking area under the doll's eyes. The nose is now decidedly "pert" and turned-up when seen in profile. The fingers are more widely separated, and thinner. The heads have no markings. The bodies are embossed with the company name, Dy-Dee and the patent numbers. The heads of dolls from Mold 3 are made of hard plastic. Their

Twenty-inch Dy-Dee Lou with painted hair from Mold 2 and her 15-inch sister, who has a caracul wig, pose for a picture in their all-original pink Effanbee coats with matching bonnets. The blue looped trim looks like a crocheted edge, but was often called lace in advertisements.

Two Dy-Dee babies are having fun in their Effanbee Dy-Dee playpen. The dolls have unusual blonde caracul wigs that look as though they have been washed and fluffed many times by a busy little doll mother.

Dressed in their Effanbee coats, these two 15-inch Mold 3 Dy-Dee babies make a pretty picture. Note the differences in the trim on the coats, as well as in the wide hat brims.

faces are less round; they appear longer and somewhat narrower than the Mold 2 faces. The painted features on the Mold 3 faces are further apart, which gives these babies a slightly older look. The painting gives the faces a slightly flat look. The eyebrows are painted well above the ridge, in a thin single-stroke curved line. The 11-inch Mold 3 doll sometimes has completely separated thin fingers. (This is true only for this size.) These same dolls have flat feet, with no separation at the big toes.

A curious example of a Mold 3 is a 15-inch doll with a very dark, almost black, caracul wig that gives it a somewhat Asian appearance. It's possible that this doll's unusual coloring and wig relate to an article in the April 1939 issue of *Playthings*, which shows a photograph of a young Chinese woman holding

Caracul wigs often begin to look a bit frazzled after repeated shampoos! This 15-inch baby with a rare blonde wig has high placement to her eyebrows, which identifies her as a Mold 3 Dy-Dee. She wears her Effanbee dotted-Swiss dress; someone has lovingly embroidered pink feather stitching at the yoke and at the hemline.

Dy-Dee Ellen stands in her original layette box, surrounded by her lovely wardrobe—all in pristine condition. This 11-inch redhead is from Mold 3.

This is a most unusual Mold 3 baby. He appears to have a black caracul wig, the only one we have seen. His complexion is very pale and he seems to have a slightly Asian look to his little face. Since Effanbee is not known to have made any Dy-Dee babies with ethnic features before 1960, this little felllow's origins remain a mystery. He is properly marked.

a Dy-Dee baby being used to demonstrate Chinese baby-care practices. Huy Ying Wu was a graduate of the Chinese Christian Hospital. She continued her studies at Cook County Hospital in Chicago, and at Mayo Clinic. Fleischaker & Baum provided her with a Dy-Dee baby, which she was allowed to dress in the traditional Chinese manner. This special Dy-Dee's hat even had jade emblems and points—to ward off evil spirits. The Dy-Dee in the

Test yourself: can you determine which head mold was used for each of these 15-inch Dy-Dee babies?

photograph in *Playthings* appears to be from Mold 1, while the one with the very dark hair, pictured in this book on the opposite page, is clearly a later doll. But perhaps that first teaching doll inspired the later black-wigged baby.

Learning to recognize the different face molds takes time and study. One help may be to "thunk" the doll's head—the rubber heads are heavier and sound different than the hard plastic heads. Examining the subtle nuances in the facial painting, however, is generally the best way to gather clues as to which mold was used to produce a particular doll.

Everyone who had the chance to play with a Dy-Dee in childhood seems to recall the unique scent of Dy-Dee's rubber body, and the delightful soft squeak her arms and legs made when moved into a new position. Effanbee developed a special system of joints for Dy-Dee's neck, arms and legs. These are called

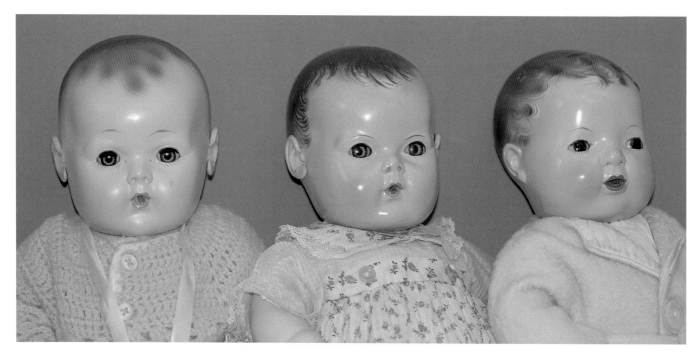

Perhaps this photograph will help with the identifications on page 41. The Dy-Dee on the far right in the white coat is from Mold 1. The Dy-Dee in the middle wearing the flowered Effanbee dress is from Mold 2. The Dy-Dee on the left in her pink bathrobe, with rather splotchy-looking hair, is from Mold 3. All of these babies are 15 inches high.

"mushroom joints" and are responsible for Dy-Dee dolls being able to float in water. Since Dy-Dee's eyes are not watertight, little girls were reminded that "good mothers never let water get into Baby's eyes." The joints fit tightly enough that Dy-Dee can be posed in many positions typical of a real infant—which further blurred the line between actual babies and this remarkable doll. If the doll's arm is raised, the jointing is secure enough to maintain that position until the child chose to change it.

In addition, Effanbee was the first company to design a tube to run from the doll's mouth to the cavity of her body. This unique mechanism permits Dy-Dee to drink from a bottle or sip from a spoon when her tummy is gently pressed, creating suction. The special valve delays

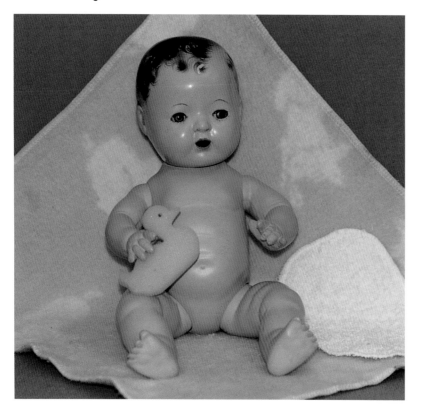

Dy-Dee dolls have beautiful baby bodies, with creases and wrinkles in all the right places.

Another mystery Dy-Dee baby, this 13-inch waif arrived in terrible condition, dressed in dirty old doll clothing and a funny straw hat. Her face is definitely from Mold 1, but she has a caracul wig. Effanbee did not put wigs on dolls until long after production of the Mold 1 Dy-Dee dolls had ended. In the process of cleaning this baby, her wig was removed, revealing that when her head was painted, the paint stopped just under the edge of the wig. The main portion of her head is unpainted hard rubber, proving that the wig is surely original to the doll. Hopefully, new information will be found one day that will solve the history of this tiny redhead with the sweet face.

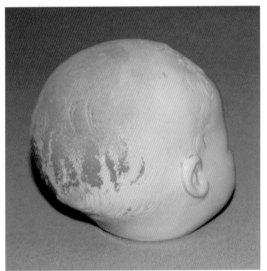

The mystery doll's head shows that the skin paint was the only color applied to her head. The remainder of her head, the portion covered by her wig, is the plain hard rubber.

A waif no more, the 13-inch mystery doll now wears her freshly laundered original dress. Her funny straw hat, not known to have ever been included in a Dy-Dee layette, has been removed and she has gained a knitted pink sweater, bonnet and booties.

Effanbee developed a unique jointing system, using what they called mushroom joints, for the dolls' arms and legs. These unusual connecting pieces allow Dy-Dee's arms and legs to operate independently.

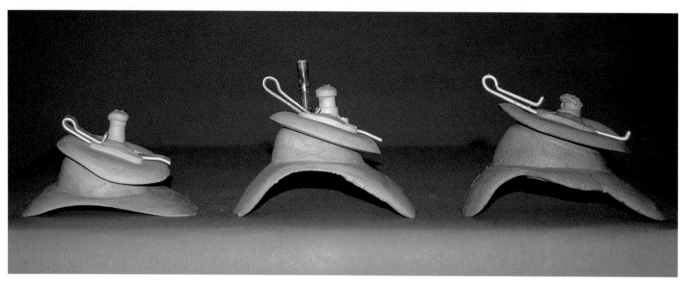

In order for Dy-Dee to float in her bath or wading pool, the joining of her head to her body, at the neck, had to be water-tight. Another style of mushroom joint was developed for this purpose. As a result, water could only enter Dy-Dee's head through her eyes, and young mothers were warned not to let this happen.

the release of the water so Dy-Dee might wait as long as fifteen minutes before wetting her diaper. The idea for a doll that could drink, then wet, just like a real baby, came from a middle-aged school teacher, Marie Wittman, who brought the idea to Hugo Baum. He immediately saw the potential of this feature for baby dolls.

Another special refinement that sets Dy-Dee apart from other dolls, even other rubber dolls, is the unique rubber surface of her body, which has an uncanny resemblance to the feel of human skin. Effanbee also took special care with the finish on the surface of the dolls' "skin." In 1937 an advertisement in the Montgomery Christmas catalog noted that "Dy-Dee feels just like a real baby—soft, smooth, and yielding; (Dy-Dee's skin is) made from the finest virgin rubber, exquisitely finished to give the impression of luscious baby skin." The rubber bodies, being substantially heavier than those made from composition and cloth, give the Dy-Dee babies a satisfying heft.

Dy-Dee was also the first baby doll designed to keep her eyes open when laid flat on her back. The unique eye mechanism developed by Effanbee also allows the doll to remain "sleeping" even when held upright. The child had only to turn the doll's head gently to the right to engage this special mechanism.

In 1940 Effanbee developed an entirely new style head for Dy-Dee, featuring flexible rubber ears, perfectly life-like, that allowed a child to learn how to clean ears with Q-tips, which were thoughtfully provided by Effanbee. In 1948 Dy-Dee came with a crier-pacifier. While a hard-plastic head was introduced in the late 1940s, Dy-Dee's body and flexible ears were still made of soft rubber. Montgomery Ward ran the last ad for an all-rubber Dy-Dee doll in 1943. This 20-inch Dy-Dee, with a trunk and complete layette, sold for twenty-one dollars.

Further enhancing the illusion that Dy-Dee was almost real was the fact that she did not immediately wet her diaper after drinking her bottle. Often she stayed dry for as long as fifteen minutes. This feat was accomplished by a unique valve system on her backside. A tube emptied from the doll's mouth into the cavity of her body, then slowly seeped out through the valve button on her rear end.

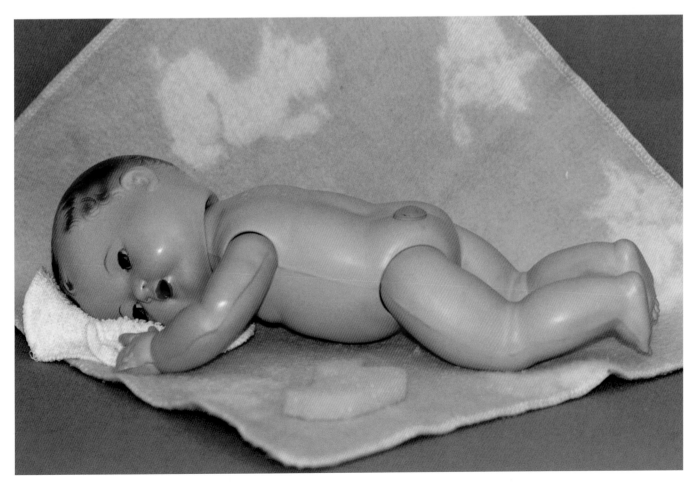

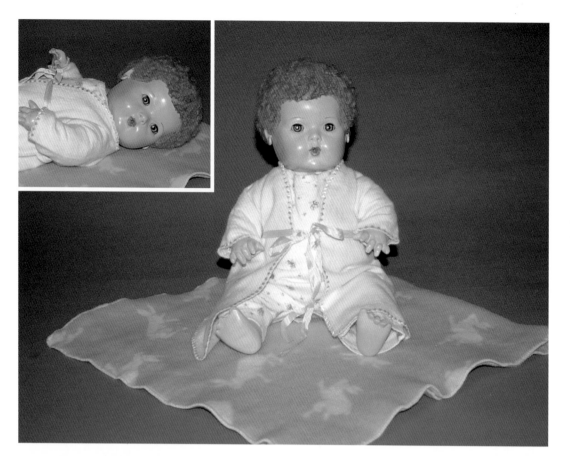

Dy-Dee, like all dolls with sleeping eyes, could keep her eyes open when she was sitting up. But unlike other dolls, Dy-Dee could also keep her eyes open when she was lying down. This was accomplished by turning her head gently to the right to engage a special mechanism designed for Effanbee.

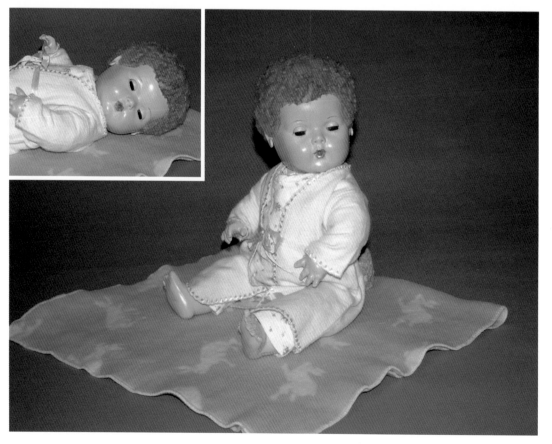

Of course Dy-Dee could close her eyes when she was put to bed for her nap, just like other dolls with sleeping eyes. But she could also remain asleep, even when she was picked up, or placed in a sitting position.

Shortages of manufacturing supplies, especially rubber, caused by war-time needs during World War II pushed doll manufacturers to rush the development of alternative materials. Thus, the military services as well as manufacturers placed a great emphasis on rapidly developing new synthetic rubbers and plastic. Although vinyl was being used in dollmaking in the late 1940s, Dy-Dee was still made with a hard-rubber head and soft-rubber body as late as 1948. The availability of these new materials, however, led to the replacement of Dy-Dee's hard-rubber head with a hard-plastic head in 1950.

Soon the soft-rubber body for which Dy-Dee was famous was replaced by one made of vinyl. In 1953 Dy-Dee came with a one-piece stuffed body and legs with disc-jointed stuffed vinyl arms. By 1956 the doll was made with a hard-plastic head and a soft-vinyl body jointed at the shoulders, hips and neck. The ears are described as rubber—by then the only part of Dy-Dee still made from this expensive material. By this year, the doll was also produced with small holes beside her nose so she could "cry" real tears. She was available with molded hair or caracul wig and sleep eyes, and with layettes and cases.

An all-vinyl version of Dy-Dee was introduced in 1967. This vinyl Dy-Dee has curled fingers and straight legs. She was offered alone or with her own teddy bear. This doll is marked "Effanbee" on her back, and she also has a golden cardboard heart hanging from her arm. Effanbee also began production of the all-vinyl doll named Dy-Dee Darlin' in 1967. These two "new" Dy-Dee dolls signaled the end of production of the heads from Molds 1, 2, and 3, which were used with the rubber bodied dolls. These new vinyl dolls bear little resemblance to the original Dy-Dee dolls. They came in 14-, 16-, 17- and 18-inch sizes. Many of these dolls do not have identification on the body, and are identified only by hang-tags on the arm. These dolls were made with molded or painted hair, molded ears and rather coarse, rooted saran-hair wigs.

In 1971 an all-vinyl Dy-Dee Educational Doll was produced by Effanbee. This 21-inch baby is rather heavy, has openings in her ears clear into the head cavity and was used by the Red Cross

An all-vinyl version of Dy-Dee was produced in 1967. She has straight legs and came dressed in a commercially knit hat, sweater and leggings in pink and white.

Effanbee also introduced a new doll to appeal to former little girls who were now mothers and grandmothers. The new doll was named Dy-Dee Darlin'. The production of this vinyl doll and the one shown on the preceding page signaled the end of the production of heads from Molds 1, 2 and 3, which were used with the rubber bodies.

to teach pre-natal baby-care classes. The doll does not resemble earlier Dy-Dees. The legs are somewhat straighter, the fingers on each hand are spread apart and she has painted hair. The head resembles those from the old Mold 3. This doll, available, with white or black skin, was offered from 1971 to 1976.

In 1973 Montgomery Ward celebrated Dy-Dee's fortieth anniversary by introducing a Dy-Dee baby, made of vinyl, but in the style of the original Mold 3 dolls. This baby came in a little white jacket and diaper set, and was tied into her display box in a pretty matching blanket. In 1984 another reissue of Dy-Dee celebrated her fiftieth anniversary. This special edition was

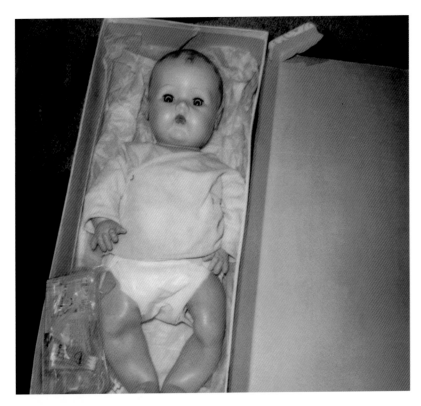

In 1971 Effanbee produced a 21-inch vinyl doll for use by the Red Cross in teaching pre-natal classes. The Dy-Dee Educational Doll has painted hair and was available with light or dark skin. The head was made from the old Mold 3.

The 1967 vinyl doll was available with a dark brunette or blonde rooted saran wig, and also came with black curly hair on a dark-skinned version of the doll.

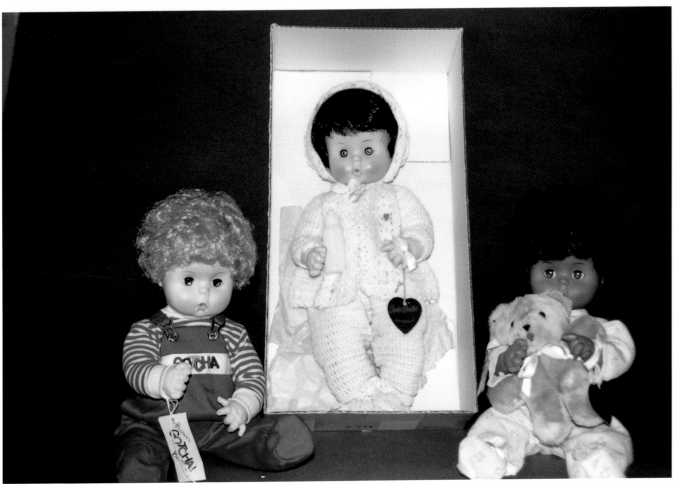

When comparing the Dy-Dee Educational Doll with vinyl head and body, to an earlier rubber-bodied doll from Mold 2, the difference in the bodies becomes apparent. The unique jointing system of the earlier Dy-Dee allows her legs to stick out in front, naturally, with only a slight curve to the leg. The vinyl doll has legs that turn outward at a rather extreme angle, so that the knees face opposite directions.

In 1984 a reiussue of Dy-dee celebreated her fiftieth anniversary. This doll wears a cotton knit undershirt and panties, and comes wrapped in a blanket. She has a hospital identification bracelet of pink-and-white beads that spells Dy-Dee.

In 2004, the seventieth anniversary of Dy-Dee, the Effanbee Doll Company, under the direction of Robert Tonner, is reissuing the 11-inch Dydee, using the Mold 1 face. For a detailed look at the creation of this doll, see chapter nine.

available with a saran wig or with molded hair. Both versions came wrapped in a blanket, dressed in cotton knit under shirt and panties, with a hospital identification style bracelet made of pink and white beads spelling "Dy-Dee."

In the 1990s Effanbee introduced another commemorative Dy-Dee, using the Mold 3 head. Made of a very dark-colored vinyl, the doll was available only in the 20-inch size and wore a knit shirt and diaper. Her presentation box held a plastic bottle with plastic nipple, blanket and toys. The quality of this doll was poor, as was that of the additional costumes—a far cry from the beautiful layettes for which Effanbee was previously known.

In 2004 Dy-Dee is once again available in a beautiful limited edition. This 11-inch baby uses the beloved Mold 1 face that was first offered in 1934. Under the direction of Robert Tonner, Effanbee is for the first time reissuing a Dy-Dee from these earliest molds. The original face is a perfect choice for the seventieth anniversary of the Dy-Dee doll.

This Dy-Dee from Mold 3 wears a homemade dress using fabrics very similar to those used by Effanbee for the clothing they made for Dy-Dee. The doll is in excellent condition and still has her large layette with many of the original items.

CHAPTER THREE

DY-DEE'S LAYETTE

Y-DEE WAS INTRODUCED in the midst of the Depression, in 1934, when not many little girls were lucky enough to receive a doll for Christmas. Elaborate Effanbee layettes were certainly beyond the means of many families. Thus there was an eager and ready market for patterns to make a complete layette for Dy-Dee at home. Butterick, McCall's and Simplicity quickly acted to serve that market. Today these patterns continue to remain popular, evoking a precious time when each new baby (or baby doll) was welcomed with a beautiful wardrobe, lovingly hand-stitched by the mother or grandmother.

Among the first patterns specified as designed for Dy-Dee was one offered by Butterick, advertised on the envelope as a "Delineator Style" pattern for Dy-Dee Baby or other baby dolls. This first pattern, Butterick #444, drawn for a 10-inch baby doll, included a shirt and diaper; a bunting with cap, which closed with the "new slide fastener" (zipper); a long coat; a frilled bonnet; a long dress with slip; a short dress with slip; a sacque; a kimono; and an embroidered bib. The pattern helpfully suggested the purchaser should buy rubber panties.

The second Butterick layette pattern, #448, included a short coat and cap; a sleeveless dressy dress with gathered neck and ribbon ties on both shoulders; a slip; a pleated romper; pajamas with buttons down the front; and the same shirt and diaper pattern as in #444. Although these two patterns from Butterick are undated, the style of the clothing suggests the mid-1930s.

In 1935 McCall's published pattern #353 for Dy-Dee dolls, which featured embroidery motifs for a little bunny and a delicate floral spray. The pattern

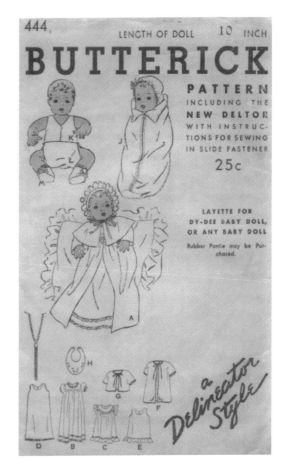

This early pattern for a Dy-Dee layette in the *Delineator Style* was issued by Butterick.

McCall's issued pattern #353 in 1935.

Pattern #513 was offered by McCall's in 1937.

included a short dress with the floral embroidery, a coat and a hat with a ruffled brim. Silk was suggested as the right fabric for the hat and coat, which have embroidery on the collar. Finally, there was a simple one-piece sun-suit with a bunny embroidered on the bib portion.

In 1937 McCall's offered pattern #513 with pieces for four outfits, including a kimono with embroidery; a satin-ribbon-edged bunting with hood; a dainty dress; a bonnet and slip with delicate floral embroidery; and a different sun-suit pattern with a duck pattern to embroider on the bib.

A longtime favorite McCall's pattern, #713, was published in 1939. Again designed specifically for Dy-Dee dolls, this pattern included a short fancy dress and a bonnet with a wide ruffled

McCall's pattern #713 was issued in 1939. It was enormously popular then, and is still avidly sought by doll collectors today.

NEW IDEAS FOR SANTA CLAUS

No. 713. The Christmas season means doll-babies for the little girl in your life, and here is a pattern for several darling outfits for the cherished Dy-Dee doll! For sizes 11, 13, 15 and 20 ins. high. Price, 25c.

No. 513. More clothes for the Dy-Dee doll, and this time there is a sweet Baby Bunting, a fluffy "best" dress and bonnet to match, a slip, kimono and a sunsuit. This pattern is for dolls 11, 13, 15 and 20 ins. high. There are many other adorable patterns for dolls' clothes in the McCall Complete Needlework Catalogue. Pattern, 25 cents.

No. 525. Dolly's clothes are as smart and up-to-date as her young mother's. These designs and several others are included, and are suitable for the "Movie" dolls, 13, 16, 18, 20, 25 ins. Pattern, 25 cents.

brim; a long dress featuring embroidery up the front; a short matching jacket with smocking; a pair of coveralls with smocking; an embroidered bib; and a flannel nightgown featuring five rows of embroidery at the neck and sweet ribbon ties at the wrists and feet. This pattern was still being featured in *McCall's Needlework & Crafts Annual,* Volume III in 1952.

An undated pattern from McCall's, #632, appears to have been the next Dy-Dee specialty pattern. The costumes included a fancy lace-trimmed sun-suit and bonnet; a beautiful short coat with lace-edged bonnet featuring a butterfly embroidery pattern; a short dress that buttons down the front, with a matching bonnet, decorated by row upon row of narrow lace; and a nightingale that uses the butterfly embroidery design again.

In 1949 McCall's offered a versatile pattern, #1493, with yet another sun-suit design, a pinafore dress with a fancy ruffled bonnet and a footed pram outfit that zipped down the front. In *McCall's Needlework & Crafts Annual* of 1952, this pattern was described as offering pieces to make clothing "Just like baby's own

Although undated, McCall's pattern #632 appears to have been drawn earlier than pattern #713, based on the style of the garments. This is the only pattern to feature the wonderful embroidered nightingale.

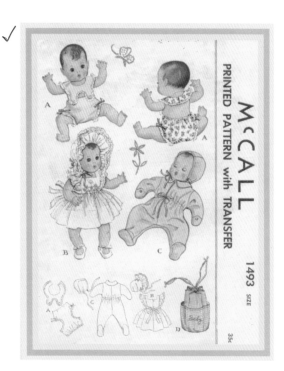

McCall's pattern #1493 was unique in offering a cleverly drawn diaper bag and a footed pram suit.

One of the patterns from #1493, made up in organdy, was featured in McCall's Needlework & Crafts Annual in 1950.

Simplicity Pattern Company also produced patterns for Dy-Dee. In their 1949 counter pattern book they featured pattern #2537, which offered a complete layette, including a blanket-stitched diaper and ribbon-tied booties. This pattern was later re-issued as Simplicity #4830.

clothes." In addition, there was a pattern to make a handy little gathered bag with pockets on the outside for holding all of the Dy-Dee doll's necessities. Although McCall's pattern #1657 from 1951 listed only Tiny Tears on the packet cover, the additional text suggested the pattern be used for Dy-Dee and all rubber-bodied baby dolls.

In 1954 McCall's published pattern #1900, which stated it was a "Ding Dong School Pattern for Tiny Tears, Dy-Dee and Kathy dolls." This interesting pattern featured a bath-time stole for the little doll mother to wear while caring for her baby doll. The stole was to be made of terrycloth and bound with bias tape. It had two deep pockets, which hung just below a child's waist.

In 1955 McCall's published pattern #2001 for a sewn and knitted layette for Dy-Dee and her "cousins," Tiny Tears and Betsy Wetsy. In the Fall-Winter 1959-60 issue of *McCall's Needlework & Crafts Magazine*, the pattern was described as: "an around-the-clock layette for baby dolls, such as Betsy Wetsy, Tiny Tears, and Dy-Dee. Wardrobe includes long and short dresses, matching slips, panties, long cape coat and bonnet, sun-suit, two-piece sleeper plus a suit, cap and booties to knit of fingering wool."

McCall's offered a much simplified pattern, #2261, for Dy-Dee, Tiny Tears and Betsy Wetsy in 1958-1959. This layette included corduroy coveralls and a percale blouse; a drawstring nightgown; a ruffled slip; a gingham dress; and a long dress, coat and bonnet. The costumes make use of bias binding at the necklines and on the sleeves. Commercially made eyelet is also used.

In May 1949 the Simplicity Pattern Company offered pattern #2537 in their May counter pattern book. The pattern

Simplicity #2659 offered an adorable layette for Dy-Dee, featuring plenty of ruffles and lace. The doll used on the pattern jacket is clearly drawn from an actual Dy-Dee doll.

In 1952 Simplicity published one of the last patterns designed especially for Dy-Dee. Number 4129 includes a long christening gown and an elegant long coat and bonnet.

was available in sizes to fit 11-, 13-, 15- and 20-inch dolls. Outfits that could be made included a tailored coat and bonnet; a fancy dress with scalloped lace edging and matching bonnet; a sun-suit and hat; a bunting with hood that fastens with satin ribbon ties; a kimono; a slip; a blanket-stitch-edged diaper; and moccasin-style booties.

Also offered in the same Simplicity counter book was pattern #2659. The doll featured was clearly drawn from a Dy-Dee baby with the Mold 2 face. This pattern included a shirt and diaper; a short dress and slip with lace edging; a nightgown; a coat and hat; a sun-suit and sun hat that is open in the back; a kimono; and a lace-trimmed sacque.

One of the last patterns to specify that it was designed for Dy-Dee was Simplicity #4129 in 1952. This pattern offered pieces to

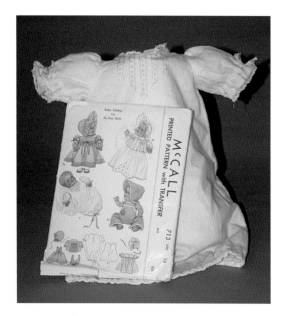

This white flannel nightgown made from McCall's pattern #713 is embellished with pink embroidery and tucking at the neckline.

Simplicity pattern #4830 was used to make this sweet batiste dress and bonnet. The dress has tiny tucking, lace edging and silk ribbon embellishment.

Lucky girls who could afford commercially made layettes could dress their dolls in Effanbee's beautiful clothing. This Dy-Dee from Mold 2 wears a silk batiste christening dress, matching long slip and deeply ruffled "portrait" bonnet, embellished with satin ribbon and fine lace, all from her original layette.

make a sun-suit with a collar; a long dress with elaborate scalloped detail on the skirt; a slip; a long coat and tailored cap; a shirt and diaper; a nightgown; a kimono; and a sacque.

In all of the patterns, every effort was made to create doll clothing that closely resembled what real babies of the era might wear. The handmade stitched and knitted outfits made from these commercial patterns are real treasures today, especially when they are found in pristine condition. They establish a valuable connection between the adult doll collectors of today and the long-ago little girls who were the first to cherish these Dy-Dee baby dolls.

For those lucky girls whose families could afford not only dolls but commercially made layettes for them, Effanbee produced beautiful doll clothing with careful craftsmanship and trims of high quality. The company was known for the high quality of their dolls, and had also developed a solid reputation for their doll clothing. The beautifully sewn baby-doll clothes were no exception to their rule of excellence. Every detail was carefully addressed. Dy-Dee's layette clothing was a far cry from the typical commercially-produced doll clothing. The finest ribbon, dainty buttons, luxurious fabrics and delicate embroideries were combined to make doll clothing fit for a tiny doll princess.

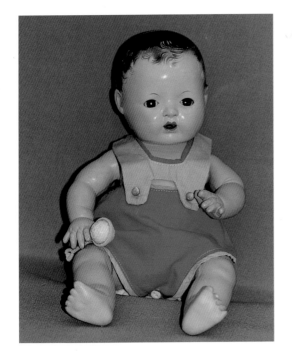

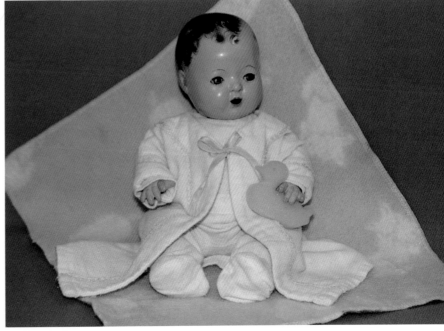

Dy-Dee-ette is ready to play in her original Effanbee sun-suit. This sun-suit style was also made up in other fabrics.

The layette items were then tucked into pretty cellophane-covered boxes.

In 1934 Effanbee began a new cycle of record sales with their Dy-Dee baby doll. Earlier they had excellent sales with their Patsy Doll Family and Shirley Temple dolls. These enormously successful dolls literally had a common thread linking them: Effanbee presented each one with an extensive beautifully

Ready for bed, this Dy-Dee from Mold 1 wears her Effanbee pajamas and flannel robe. The robe is embroidered in pink. The 11-inch baby sits on an Esmond Mills bunny blanket.

Effanbee boxed layette sets were very complete, including everything a doll mother might need to care for her baby. In this example, an organdy dress and bonnet are packaged with a satin hair bow, oil-cloth shoes, rayon socks, a batiste slip and specially marked Dy-Dee bubble bath.

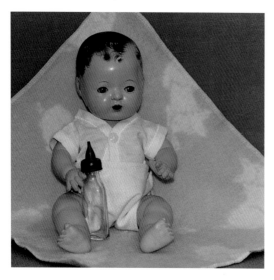

All Dy-Dee dolls came in a shirt and diaper. On some dolls the shirt was made of mercerized-cotton knit and buttoned in the front. Others wore a rayon knit undershirt that simply pulled over the doll's head. This baby also holds her original Dy-Dee nursing bottle with the rubber nipple still intact.

These are two versions of the early embroidered-collar Effanbee dress, which was offered in a long and a short length. The Dy-Dee wearing the short dress also has original shoes.

Dainty dotted-Swiss was a favorite fabric for use in Dy-Dee dresses. In this example, the butterfly sleeves have been gathered up at the shoulder and tied with silk bows. The crown portion of the double-frilled organdy ruffle-edged bonnet is made of dotted-Swiss. The model is an early 15-inch Dy-Dee.

made wardrobe of clothing that looked just like what real little girls and babies were wearing.

In *The Patsytown News*, Volume 1, Number 3, published in 1934, the first detailed description of a Dy-Dee layette was given in a sub-section of text entitled "Dy-Dee Has Pretty Things." This first layette included dresses; slips; bonnets; a bathrobe and wrappers of every description; cotton shirts; Birdseye diapers; rubber pants; woolen crib blankets; percale crib sheets; face cloths; nipples; bottles; soap; talcum powder; and little packages of absorbent cotton. In addition, there were knitted booties and leatherette shoes with rayon socks.

Advertisements for Dy-Dee explained that: "Only Effanbee, famous for more than 25 years as makers of the finest quality dolls, can create such perfection. Finest virgin rubber, exquisitely finished, gives the effect of luscious baby skin." In italics, the ads stated that Dy-Dee's unique drinking and wetting feature was under patent by Effanbee. Mothers were warned: "When your little girl asks for a Dy-Dee, give her the genuine— and not a substitute for which she'll have to apologize."

Early Dy-Dee dresses often had a loose cap-sleeve which was referred to as a "butterfly" sleeve. These sleeves were found on everyday dresses, as well as more elaborate christening dresses. These two dolls are from Mold 1.

This 20-inch Dy-Dee Louise from Mold 2 is wearing an everyday pink cotton dress and bonnet and the early moccasin-style shoes, which were made of a soft leather-like material.

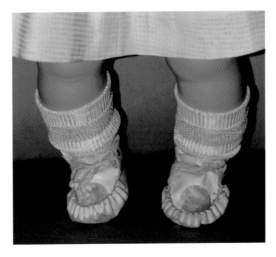

A close-up of the shoes shows the pink-and-white pompoms on the toes. Shoes in this style were made for all sizes of Dy-Dee. Pink trimmed socks complete the outfit.

Twenty-inch Dy-Dee Lou from Mold 1 wears a green-dotted white dimity dress that brings out her green eyes. The dress is gathered at the sides with tucks to give it a nicer fit. The bonnet, dress, shoes and bottle are all part of this doll's original layette.

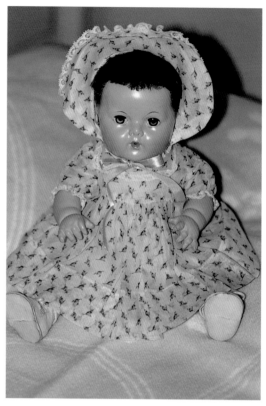

A favorite dress fabric for Dy-Dee is this blue sprigged voile, fetchingly worn by a 15-inch Dy-Dee from Mold 2. She also wears her original Effanbee tie-shoes made of leatherette. The bunny blanket in the background was made by Esmond Mills.

Original Dy-Dee clothing is often found in dreadful condition, as are some of the dolls. This sweet-faced Mold 2 Dy-Dee was literally in pieces when found wrapped in a box with what appeared to be very dirty scraps of fabric. After a thorough washing, these revealed themselves to be the doll's original flowered dimity dress. The bonnet, made of window-pane dimity, did not at first appear to match the dress. However, searching through old catalogs established that the hem-stitched bonnet does, indeed, go with this dress. The doll also cleaned up very nicely. No one would guess she spent years in a dirty old cardboard box!

An entire chapter could be written about the many coats and winter-wear that were created for Dy-Dee. These two babies from Mold 1 wear similar short coats and bonnets. The one on the left wears the pink silk taffeta coat with delicate blue embroidery; the little white coat on the other doll is linen with no embellishment.

This Dy-Dee from Mold 3 is a picture of pink perfection in her all-original organdy dress and bonnet. Even the satin ribbons are in pristine condition.

Some Dy-Dee dolls simply insist on being boys. This little fellow is wearing a white wool flannel coat with a belt and three large pearl buttons. His matching knit cap was added to keep his ears warm.

Dy-Dee is all set for play in her smocked blue-and-white checked cotton dress. She wears original shoes. Her reddish wig has the suggestion of a widow's peak and her high eyebrows show that she is a 15-inch doll from Mold 3.

For those not familiar with the garment called a "nightingale," it is essentially a blanket with one corner gathered to create a hood. The blanket is then wrapped around the baby. McCall's pattern #632 offered instructions to make a nightingale.

A blue-and-white nightingale shows how well it works to keep this Mold 1 Dy-Dee warm.

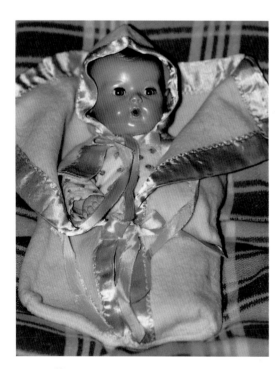

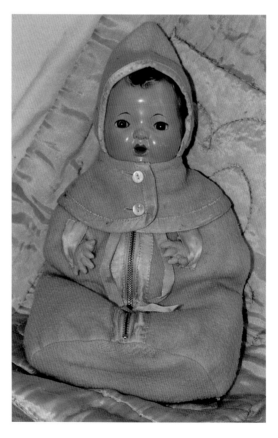

This Mold 1 Dy-Dee wears an Effanbee wool bunting with peaked cap, zipper front, a unique opening for the hands and a cowl that buttons under the chin for extra protection.

Some Effanbee buntings close with silk ribbon ties. This one features a separate hood that ties under the chin. This 11-inch Dy-Dee from Mold 2 is also wearing Effanbee flannel pajamas with a pink-and-blue print.

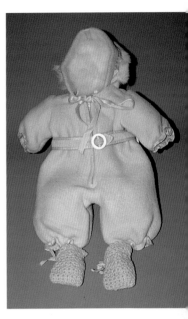

A group of Dy-Dee triplets is all ready for the first snow storm. Mold 1 Dy-Dee, left, wears a pink wool snow-suit with white angora trim and a pearl belt buckle at the waist. She even has little mittens for her hands. Mold 2 Dy-Dee, center, wears a blue snow-suit that zips up the front and snaps at the waist. Mold 3 Dy-Dee, right, wears a later snow-suit with a white-trimmed belt at the waist. She has knitted white mittens.

The paratrooper-style snow-suit worn by the Mold 1 Dy-Dee in the photo at left is all one piece, with a separate belt. The hood ties at the neck. Booties have been added to keep her feet warm.

The yellow of this eiderdown coat and hat is a perfect color for this red-headed 11-inch Dy-Dee from Mold 3.

This interesting Effanbee bunting is a bit like a blanket with sleeves. In this version, the baby's head fits low inside a deep collar. There are no closures; the bunting is to be wrapped tightly around Dy-Dee, then folded up from the bottom to cover her legs. This Mold 3 baby demonstrates what may be a problem as she sticks out her bare feet!

Brother and sister Dy-Dee dolls are wearing their brightly colored knitted play-sets. Effanbee used bright colors such as red and vivid blue in many of the first Dy-Dee layettes.

There were many darling knitted and crocheted pieces made for Dy-Dee, too. This pink set includes a cap with tassels, a sweater and booties.

The ad shows a smiling little girl preparing to change her Dy-Dee doll's diapers. This doll came dressed simply in a mercerized-cotton shirt and Birdseye diaper. A layette for the doll was sold separately. Included in the layette set, which came packed in a sturdy cardboard case with a carrying handle, were an organdy dress; a slip; rubber pants; a bib; a shirt; a blanket; a washcloth; a crib pad; a rubber sheet; two diapers; two powder puffs; cotton; pins; soap; powder; and a bottle with nipple. Layettes were available for three sizes of Dy-Dee dolls: 20 inches, 14 1/2 inches and 11 inches.

On another page of the 1936 Montgomery Ward Christmas catalog, a luxury edition of Dy-Dee was offered with a complete layette, all packaged in a trunk case "specially for good little girls." Included in this layette were a long organdy dress; a net-trimmed organdy bonnet; a mercerized shirt; a Birdseye diaper; rubber pants; and a white sleeping garment with a drop seat. Of course, there is a bottle and rubber nipple, too. This case is covered with pink-and-white paper and has a separate tray that could be lifted out. The doll fits perfectly on a pad in the top tray portion. These sets were available for the same three Dy-Dee sizes.

In 1937 a thirty-piece layette was offered by Montgomery Ward in their Christmas catalog. Priced at $1.79, the decorated hinged box's contents included a batiste dress; a lawn slip;

a flannel blanket; a crib pad; two Birds-eye diapers; a mercerized shirt; rubber pants; twelve safety pins; two Birdseye belly bands; a rubber sheet; a wash cloth; three powder puffs; a sponge; a hot water bottle; soap; baby powder; a Dy-Dee logo bottle and rubber nipple; clothes pins and a line.

The extensive layette collections, coupled with furniture and baby care equipment, helped little girls create a magical nursery world for themselves and their dolls. The layettes and dolls were housed in wonderful trunk-like cases that featured colorful graphics, drawers and lift-out trays. The Dy-Dee baby doll rested in the top tray, which contained a pad with a pretty ruffled organdy edge. The clothing and accessories were in the deep portion of the trunk, under the tray. Some trunks had drawers, into which were tucked some of the smaller items. Going through one of these trunks laden with goodies for Dy-Dee was the ultimate treasure hunt for little girls who loved dolls.

In 1939 Montgomery Ward offered a nineteen-piece layette for Dy-Dee for $1.89. Included were a white batiste dress with embroidered collar and lace trim; a batiste bonnet; a lawn slip; pajamas and a wrapper made of printed cotton flannel; a mercerized shirt; a pink eider-down bathrobe and booties; a blanket; a crib pad; two Birdseye diapers; a feeding spoon; a Dy-Dee bottle with a rubber nipple sized to fit Dy-Dee's mouth; safety pins; a wash cloth; rubber panties; and an Effanbee booklet entitled "What Every Young Doll Mother Should Know."

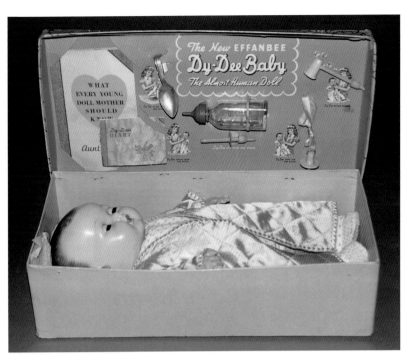

Placing the accessories in the lid is a very efficient way to present Dy-Dee and her necessities. This Mold 3 example is wearing her luxurious satin quilted robe.

Effanbee made glass bottles in several different styles over the years of Dy-Dee's production. This is the narrow-necked bottle with a dark-red nipple on the outside of the rim.

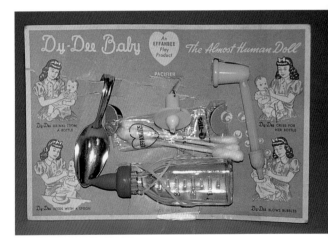

One of the accessory sets familiar to Dy-Dee collectors is sometimes found in the lid of the doll's box, with the accessories stitched to the light cardboard. The set was also included in layette sets and trunks. All of the Dy-Dee essentials are here: spoon; pacifier; bubble pipe; glass-logo nursing bottle; and Q-tips made for Effanbee.

Many of these layettes include a vast array of clothing. Different fabrics were used to create clothing with innovative designs. The tremendous variety of outfits meant Dy-Dee had special outfits for every activity. The costumes for this baby from Mold 1 include fancy dresses with bonnets; sleepwear; a bunting; a sweater; caps; booties; mittens; soakers; a christening dress; a long silk taffeta coat; a printed play dress; and sun-suits.

The Mold 1 Dy-Dee layettes often included belly bands of soft flannel and a "pinning blanket," seen in the foreground. In the far left, there is a pair of pink "rubber" pants, which was a standard layette item.

A thirteen-piece layette in a pretty gift box was offered by Montgomery Ward in 1941. This collection included a long white batiste dress, with box pleats and lace at cuffs and neck; a matching bonnet with pink satin streamers; a white slip; a soft, fleecy cotton flannel blanket; a mercerized cotton shirt; a Birds-eye diaper; rubber pants; a pink cotton flannel bathrobe with embroidered hood and silk tie; footed pajamas with drop seat and buttons with buttonhole closure; a wash cloth; twelve safety pins; absorbent cotton; and Q-tips.

In the same catalog, Montgomery Ward offered a Dy-Dee with a full layette that included a blue-and-white dress and bonnet that fastens with buttons and buttonholes; a Birdseye diaper; a cotton flannel jacket; a slip; rayon socks; white imitation-leather shoes; a bathrobe; striped pajamas with drop seat and button closure; an extra diaper; a mercerized cotton shirt; rubber pants; a cotton flannel blanket; cotton; talcum powder; safety pins;

Most of the Dy-Dee layette collections could be purchased in predominantly blue or pink. This pretty collection belongs to a 15-inch doll from Mold 1.

An amazing early complete and original layette belongs to this 20-inch Dy-Dee with sparkling green eyes from Mold 1.

soap; foaming bubble bath; Q-tips; and a Dy-Dee nursing bottle with rubber nipple, bubble pipe and spoon. The doll and layette were packaged in a fiber-board case with a leather handle.

Also in this catalog from 1941, the Dy-Dee Baby Bathinette was offered for $1.89. The description states that the Bathinette was especially designed for Dy-Dee dolls. These doll Bathinettes were built in the same factory that made Bathinettes for real babies.

Each year some items in Dy-Dee's layette remained the same, but there were always new additions to excite prospective Dy-Dee mamas. For example, early coat and hat combinations were made of silk or taffeta, edged with fine lace and enhanced with embroidery. In 1948 a sturdy cotton lace-trimmed hat and coat were added to the layette. This lace appears to be more like hand-made tatting, but Effanbee described it as lace. In this set, the dress was made in dainty dotted-Swiss fabric. The ensemble remained popular through the 1940s and 1950s.

Throughout the production of Dy-Dee, little knit sweaters, caps, booties, mittens and scarves were offered, usually in pink and white, but sometimes in blue and white. Some of the sweater sets appear to have been crocheted rather than knitted.

In 1955 layette items included with Dy-Dee Jane were a plastic bottle with rigid plastic nipple; two powder puffs; a bath sponge;

This lucky Mold 2 Dy-Dee has a blue coat and hat for everyday, and a much fancier pink silk taffeta set for dressier occasions. She also has a white pinafore dress and bonnet, deep blue rubber pants, a pink robe with an appliquéd kitty pocket and an assortment of pretty dresses.

Wonderful fabrics and costumes were included in this Mold 2 Dy-Dee's layette. She has a long christening gown with bonnet; a pink coat and hat with blue loop fringe; a white dotted-Swiss dress; a yellow-sprigged white dimity dress and bonnet; a bunting with front zipper closure; and a cotton dress and bonnet in blue-flowered fabric. The doll wears the familiar Effanbee pink-and-white dress.

a satin-edged pink blanket; Q-tips; a plastic straw with a pink tip; a plastic bubble pipe, Kleenex; a "silver" spoon; a baby record book; and the doll care instruction book. This Dy-Dee has a gold heart-shaped cardboard tag that introduces her as "Dy-Dee Jane." The tag also states she could weep real tears. The doll wears a mercerized-cotton knit shirt, white-with-red polka-dot flannel

This 15-inch Dy-Dee must be very proud of all her matching dresses and hats. She also has a very brightly colored sun-suit and Dy-Dee Logo pajamas and robe as well as a blue coat and hat.

This 15-inch Dy-Dee from Mold 3 will be nice and warm with all her cozy cover-ups. She has a particularly beautiful satin quilted robe (left) and an unusual red version of the familiar cotton coat and bonnet.

New items in the layette for this 15-inch Dy-Dee from Mold 3 include pink coveralls and a tee-shirt (right) and a pink sun-suit with large white floral design. She is wearing an embroidered-yoke sundress and a matching bonnet.

diaper, a "hospital" bead bracelet and white rayon socks.

Other highly desirable layette items were the wonderful blankets of various styles that accompanied Dy-Dee. One of the most eagerly sought-after layette items is the bunny blanket made by the Esmond Mills, circa 1930. These blankets had reversible designs woven into the soft fabric. They came in pink or blue. Esmond Mill also made blankets featuring hearts, cherubs and the words: "Dy-Dee Baby." (In 2003, two of these little blankets sold at auction for $89.99.) Other blankets were made of a thinner cotton flannel edged with satin binding or blanket stitching. Some had delicate embroidery as well.

Each year brought new accessory and layette items for Dy-Dee. Effanbee wisely offered the dolls alone, the dolls complete with a layette and layettes without the doll. Some of the Dy-Dee outfits were packaged for individual sales. The company thus augmented the sale of new dolls with continuing sales of clothing and accessories.

The Dy-Dee Feeding Set came in a decorated pink-and-blue

This Mold 2 Dy-Dee wears a christening dress and has some new items in her layette. There is a pinning blanket made of Dy-Dee Logo cotton flannel on which rests an accessory set. The pinning blankets are most often found in plain white flannel. There is also a white blouse and blue-print skirt with shoulder straps as well as a red-and-white checked romper for playtime fun.

Some lucky little girl received this luxury Dy-Dee gift set from FAO Schwarz years ago. The doll came in a pink box with silvery-white stars all over it, and lies on a lovely organdy-edged pillow. This special edition set also included an embroidered quilt. Note the Dy-Dee shoes: they were originally white, but as the leatherette ages, it turns rather brittle and yellow. It is important to know what the shoes look like today, so that they can be correctly identified when found.

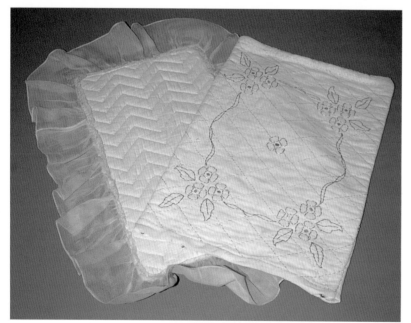

This close-up of the embroidered quilt may suggest a project for today's Dy-Dee mothers who quilt and embroider for their dolls.

box with graphics of a little girl feeding her baby doll. The box was 5 x 6 3/4 x 2 1/2 inches and contained a pink plastic cup, a vinyl bib and a silver spoon. (In 2003, an example of this set sold for more than $117.)

Another clever accessory was the Dy-Dee Utility Kit, so marked in navy-blue print on the outside of a pink plastic zippered bag that measured 10 x 7 inches with a 28-inch strap. The original set included an assortment of Dy-Dee necessities.

Among the special accessory sets made by Effanbee was a "Dy-Dee's Mother Outfit," which was pictured in the John Plein catalog of 1938. This little set was contained in a tan cardboard suitcase with red stripes. It had a brass closure and a red "leather" padded handle, and held a hot water bottle; a white uniform apron and cap; a rubber apron; a nursing bottle; powder puffs; a washcloth; and a Dy-Dee Diary

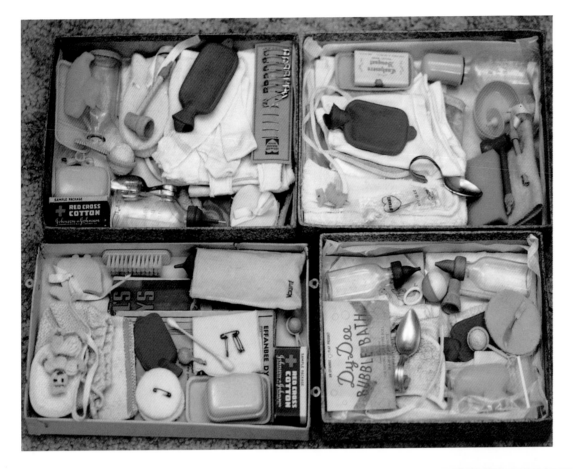

Dy-Dee accessories were tucked neatly into the drawers of the layette cases.

Wonderful accessory sets helped little girls create a special world in which to care for their Dy-Dee babies. This array of useful items was included with various Effanbee boxed sets, and suggests how extensive the accessory collections were.

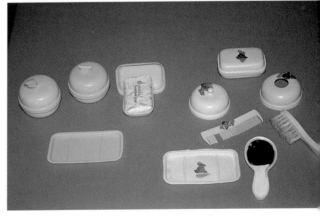

Celluloid, and later hard-plastic, doll-care sets were packaged with Dy-Dee layettes. This set is bright pink; it also came in a deep-blue color. Another set was made in ivory with a little green and red holly design.

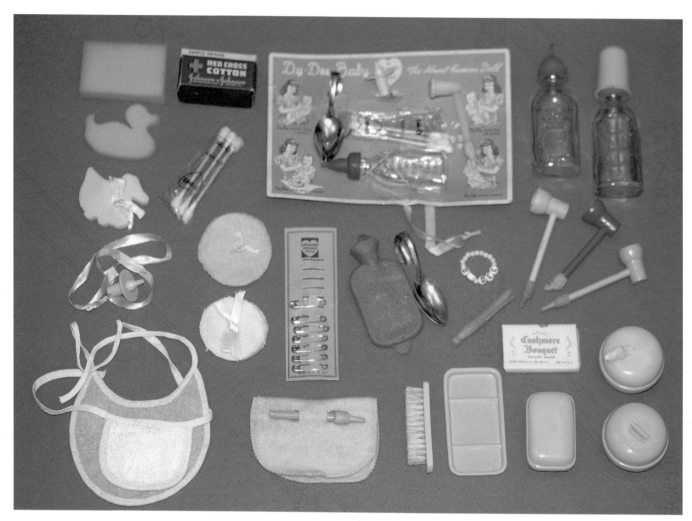

This arrangement shows the variations in the standard accessory items you may find when at a doll show or auction. These items were all included in various Dy-Dee sets over a long period of time.

This is an example of an unusual early Dy-Dee nursing bottle from Effanbee. The rubber nipple actually fits tightly down into the neck of the bottle for feeding the doll. On later bottles the rubber nipples fit over the glass rim of the bottle.

Of course, if Dy-Dee was to be fed properly, her bottles needed to be washed and "sterilized," just like a real baby's. This is a metal sterilizer with wire rack and its full set of glass bottles and nipples. The metal pot, by Amsco, also came in a kelly-green color. It is not known if Effanbee actually sold these sets, or if they were simply created to fill a need by another quick-thinking company.

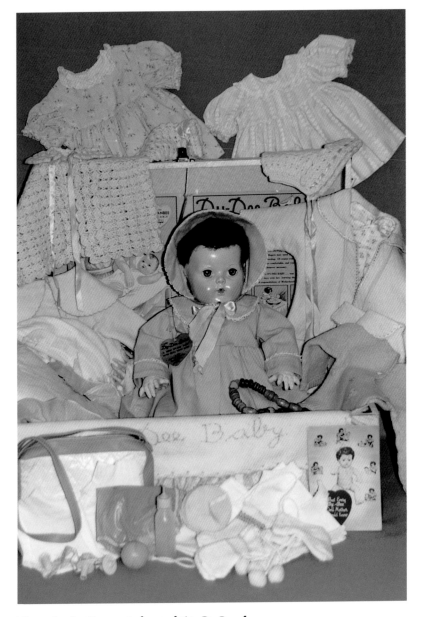

The quilted utility set in front of this Dy-Dee from Mold 2 is not an "official" Dy-Dee set, but it was sold in Montgomery Ward catalogs on the same page as Dy-Dee, so it is often included as "original" when Dy-Dee is sold on the secondary market.

The Dy-Dee Feeding Set is difficult to find today. It makes a wonderful accessory for Dy-Dee's mealtimes.

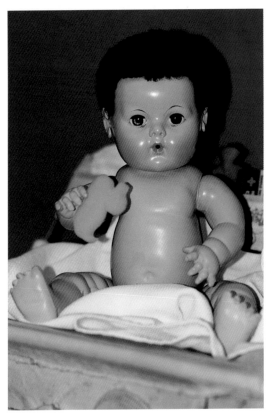

The yellow duck sponge is a favorite Dy-Dee accessory. It is frequently found because this bath-time essential was included with many Dy-Dee layette sets, even those not including the doll.

with a pencil. The suitcase measured 12 3/4 x 14 1/2 x 4 1/2 inches. The colorful graphics on the inside of the lid showed a little girl feeding her Dy-Dee baby. (This set sold in 2003 for more than $60.)

Effanbee also made boxed Doctor and Nurse sets. Although these sets did not specifically mention Dy-Dee, the accompanying illustrations showed a little boy or girl caring for a Dy-Dee doll.

This 11-inch molded-hair doll with brown eyes is from Mold 3. She wears a white christening dress with a lace-edged trim on the bottom of the yoke, as well as a white slip and ivory hand-knit bonnet and sweater.

CHAPTER FOUR

CASES, TRUNKS & FURNITURE

A GREAT DEAL OF ATTENTION was given to the packaging of Dy-Dee dolls and their wardrobes. From the very beginning, the trunks, boxes and cases in which the dolls were sold were sturdy and attractive. The inside of the lids were illustrated with colorful graphics of little girls caring for their Dy-Dee babies. The exteriors were covered with heavy, textured paper, ranging from pink and white to gold and white, ivory, a mottled red with ivory or pink, plain ivory and beige with a center red stripe. Designs on the exterior included stars and a snowflake/flower design. Later boxes had solid pink bottoms and a gold and pink cloud design on ivory. One of the later cases was made to resemble a sewing machine tote, with a hard-plastic outer shell.

Effanbee produced a variety of interiors for the Dy-Dee boxes. One of the boxes featured two rectangular spaces: one for the doll, the other for her layette. This style of box was also made somewhat deeper in height to accommodate anywhere from one to five drawers, which could be pulled out with little metal handles. In one modest box, Dy-Dee was laid flat on top of her layette. Inside the lid, in addition to the graphic design, there were little elastic loops to hold her spoon, bottle, bubble pipe, pacifier and diary.

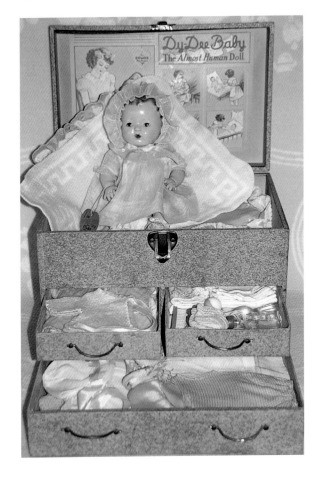

The elaborate cases that were produced for Dy-Dee contributed to the doll's allure. This multi-drawer version is the perfect setting for this Mold 1 baby.

CASES, TRUNKS & FURNITURE • 81

There were almost as many styles of layette cases as there were layette clothing items. One of the more remarkable cases appears to have been an adaptation of a hard-sided sewing-machine case.

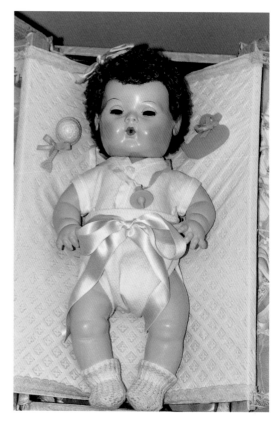

Large Dy-Dee layette trunks had as many as three pull-out drawers. This example has two narrow drawers and one that is the full-width of the trunk to accommodate the doll's layette. The doll is from Mold 1 and is dressed as a boy in an ivory woolen coat.

This doll from Mold 3 is in perfect condition, thanks in part to the hard-plastic outer shell of her case, shown above and on the opposite page.

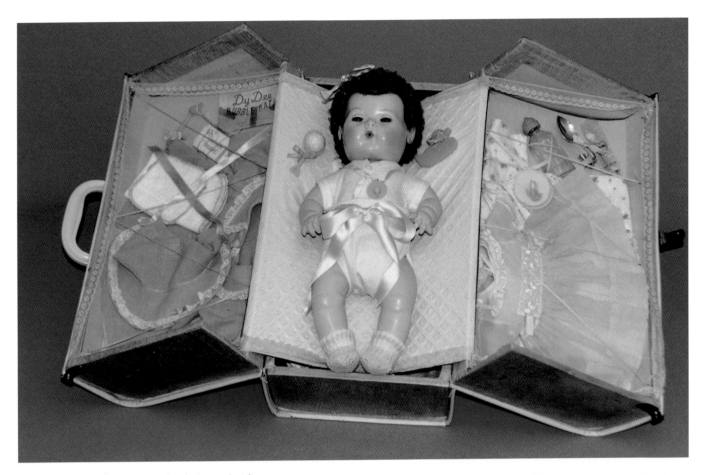

The outer shell of this case is hard plastic. Inside, a Mold 3 Dy-Dee doll, with her layette and accessory items evenly distributed on either side of the center compartment, rests on a quilted pink "hammock." This case was used to present a regular layette collection with well-made clothing, including the traditional blue coat with white lace trim, and various bath and feeding items.

The simplest Dy-Dee boxes were just large enough to hold the doll and have the same exterior paper coverings and interior graphics as the elaborate cases. Even on these simple boxes, the lids were attached with a piece of twill tape to prevent loss or destruction of the lid.

A case of a later style had a space for Dy-Dee and her hard accessory pieces, such as her bottle, pacifier, bubble pipe, Q-tips, etc. in the base. The clothing was attached with stitches to the inside of the lid. These cases, which opened for display like a book, did not have graphics inside the lid.

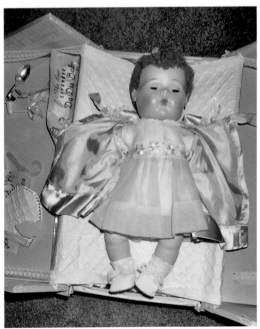

An earlier example of the case shown above was clearly well-loved. The doll in this case wears a luxurious blue satin coat over a pink organdy dress. The case holds an assortment of other clothing and basic accessory pieces.

The exterior of this case has a plain pink base and colorful design of gold and pink swirls on a white lid.

Mold 1 Dy-Dees with blonde hair are particularly hard to find. This one wears her original Effanbee dotted-Swiss dress with butterfly sleeves and her soft-leather booties. Inside the lid of the Dy-Dee box is an early simple graphic, which was repeated on the doll-care brochures.

Another interesting case opens like a book and has a space for Dy-Dee and her hard accessories on one side, with her extra layette items on the other side.

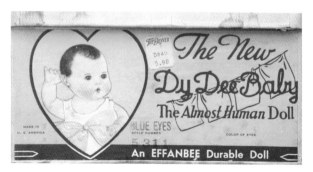

Even when the doll was in a simple box with no accoutrements, the graphics on the end of the box promised a wonderful surprise inside.

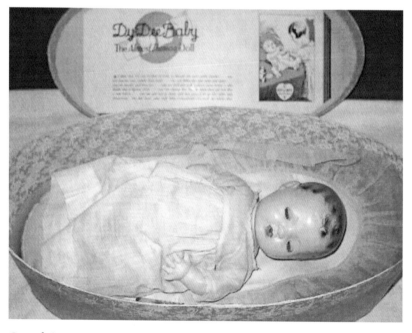

One of the rarest Dy-Dee cases is this oval one with a Mold 1 doll inside. This box is similar to the one Effanbee used for the Lamkin baby doll in 1930, but is clearly meant for Dy-De. The graphics inside the lid are the typical Dy-Dee graphics, and the normal rectangular quilted pad with organdy ruffle has been adapted to an oval shape for this presentation of a 1934 Dy-Dee.

This elaborate presentation case has multi-layered pull-out side wings filled with Dy-Dee goodies. The doll is beautifully displayed in front of a mirror that is glued into the underside of the case lid.

One quite elaborate case opened to reveal a triptych: the center space held the doll; matching spaces on either side held layette items. Additional trays matching the layette space folded out and contained even more clothing. The center space, where Dy-Dee lay, had a flip-up lid that holds a mirror.

One extremely rare presentation box was made in an oval shape, reminiscent of the unusual oval box Effanbee used for their Lamkin baby doll in 1930. However, the oval case used with a Mold 1 Dy-Dee was certainly issued with this doll—the colorful early graphics showing a little girl caring for her Dy-Dee were printed inside the lid, just as in later, more traditional, rectangular trunks and cases. The doll rested inside the box on an oval ruffle-trimmed pillow.

A 20-inch Mold 1
Dy-Dee sits inside the
top of her elaborate
presentation case. Each
drawer is packed with
Dy-Dee necessities and
there is a ruffled pad
with a soft pillow and
quilts, on which the doll
may recline, in the top
portion of the case.

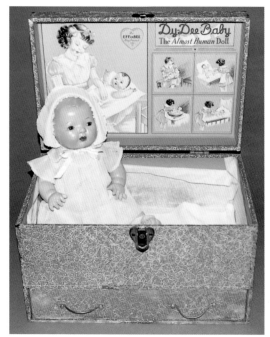

Cases with many variations in configuration
and outer covering were issued by Effanbee
with their Dy-Dee babies. This two-drawer
case is home to a Mold 1 Dy-Dee. Note the
mottled red-and-ivory exterior.

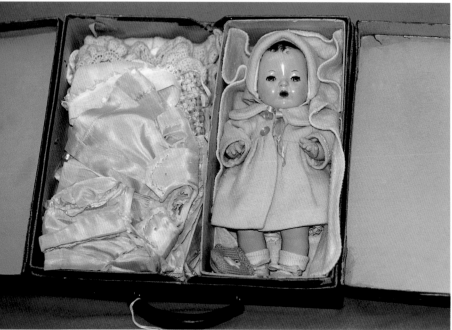

This unusual case was made for the Mold 1 Dy-Dee.
The doll reclines in a narrow compartment, and next
to her is a wider section to hold her layette. The
uneven sides are covered by lids that fasten, and the
whole case can be carried upright by its handle.

Rarely do we find a Mold 1 Dy-Dee in un-played-
with condition, such as this 13-inch baby in a pink
presentation case. Her accessories and layette are
still pristine under their original cellophane covering.

The unusual yellow graphics on this box were also used inside the oval box shown on the bottom of page 84. This set, with the lovely crocheted blanket and a Mold 1 Dy-Dee holding her bottle, are part of the luxury presentation set offered exclusively at FAO Schwarz.

A much simplified display box was used for this 20-inch Dy-Dee Louise from Mold 3. There are no interior graphics and her hard accessory pieces are attached to the side of the box. The doll came dressed in a white cotton coat and bonnet with blue trim and booties. She is wrapped in a satin-ribbon-edged blue blanket and tied into the box.

When Effanbee introduced the new Dy-Dee with applied rubber ears, they also introduced a new graphic design that emphasized this unique Dy-Dee feature.

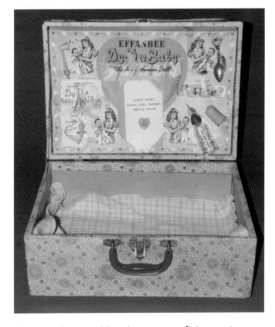

The largest layette trunks were quite elaborate. When the lid was raised, a bed area for Dy-Dee was created. Dy-Dee rested on a quilted pad edged with a pretty organdy ruffle. Below this space, a variety of little drawers could be pulled out to reveal additional clothing and accessories for the doll.

In 1953 Dy-Dee came in a luggage-style case, with her clothing

This case has a gold-and-ivory snowflake swirl design as well as a newer yellow background graphic design in the lid. If you look closely, you can see that the doll's bubble pipe, pacifier, nursing bottle, bottle cap and spoon are all attached to the graphic design in the lid.

The Bathinette is one of the most difficult Dy-Dee items to find in mint condition. The set comes in a large square red box with a familiar Effanbee graphic on the inside of the lid.

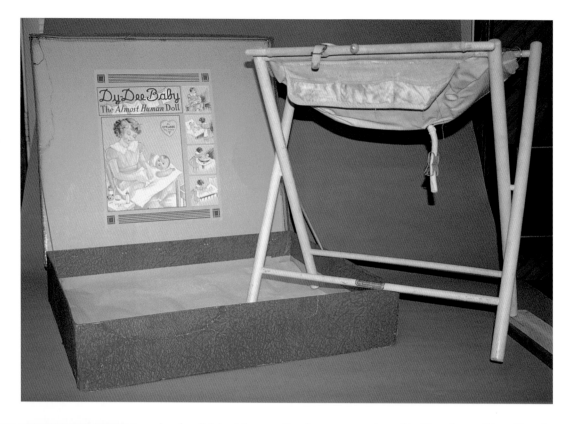

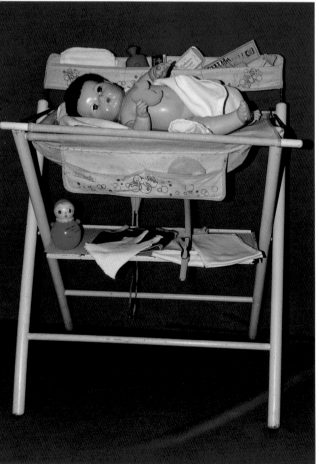

in the lid inside a cellophane covering. Dy-Dee herself reclined in a little cardboard cradle that fit perfectly inside the lower portion of the case.

In 1954 Dy-Dee could be purchased in a "clearvue playpen box." She was dressed in a shirt and diaper, but her little flannel pajamas were included in the box, as were her accessories: a bottle; a bubble pipe; a pacifier; a feeding spoon; a sipping straw; and Q-tips.

Effanbee also offered an extensive line of furniture with which a child could create a complete little domestic world. The first item of furniture made expressly for Dy-Dee was the Bathinette, an exact copy of the same essential bathing and diapering table made for real babies. The Bathinette was advertised extensively with Effanbee Dy-Dee, beginning in 1935 and continuing for years. The Bathinette features a rubberized fabric tub with a hose at the bottom for draining water. The wooden

When the top of the Bathinette is closed over the tub, a handy changing table is created. A rubber hose with a metal clamp allows water to be easily drained from the tub portion.

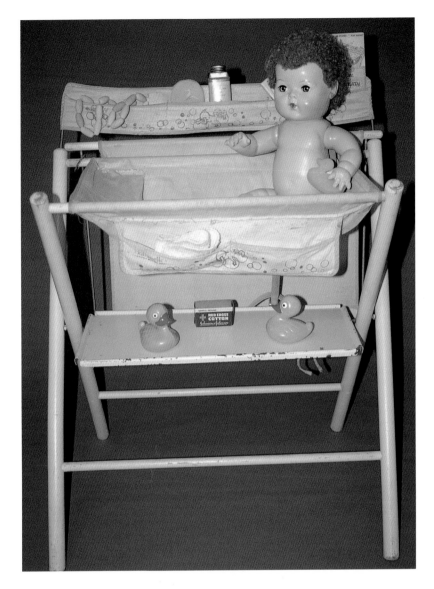

Dy-Dee obviously enjoys her bath in her authentically detailed Bathinette. This version has cloth pockets above and along the back of the tub to hold bath-time essentials. There is also a handy metal shelf between the wooden legs for storing Dy-Dee's bath toys or clean clothing.

support pieces were enameled in ivory at the same factory that made Bathinettes for real babies. An "apron" with storage pockets on the front and a pocket on the top were ready to store soap, powder, pins, a wash cloth, etc. Between baths, the tub part could be covered by a lid that fit over the tub to form a dressing table, complete with a fastening strap to keep "the little rascal from wiggling off!" This ingenious piece of equipment was a co-operative effort between Effanbee and the Bathinette Company. By 1941 Sears Roebuck and other catalogs were carrying imitation Bathinettes, such as the Doll-E-Bath.

Of course Dy-Dee needed a bed. Since these pieces were not marked with either the Effanbee name, or Dy-Dee, it is difficult to state with certainty which pieces were, in fact, sold as official

Although this deep-pink wicker cradle is shown in Effanbee photos it may not have been designed specifically for Dy-Dee.

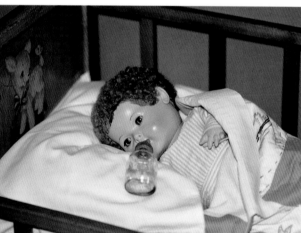

This maple crib features a typical nursery decal, circa 1950. The baby is a Mold 3 Dy-Dee, drinking her bottle.

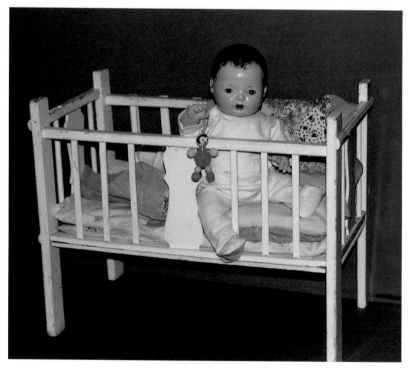

This 15-inch Dy-Dee from Mold 1 does not look ready for sleep. The white wooden crib is contemporary to the doll, but the manufacturer is not identified.

Dy-Dee furniture. Effanbee offered wicker-type cradles for baby dolls for a number of years. The deep-pink version was probably made expressly for Dy-Dee. But even when furniture was identified with the Dy-Dee name, the advertising material often went on to promote that it could be used for "other baby dolls." The Dy-Dee playpen had colorful pink and blue paint and featured a cardboard "pad" in a brown-and-ivory diamond pattern.

One item that is well-documented is Dy-Dee's buggy. This luxurious carriage had strong springs, rubber-tired wheels and an oil-cloth hood that could be collapsed, in addition to a metal-and-wooden carriage bed for the doll. The buggy featured elegant art-deco-style graphics on the sides. Another typical carriage of Dy-Dee's era was made of tightly woven wicker, with a hood and back-rest, which allowed the doll to sit up for

An early maple-wood playpen may have been ordered by Effanbee. The playpen is usually found with casters at the four corners. On this one, the casters have been replaced with beads.

Dy-Dee playpens were made of wood and came with pink and blue or red and bright-blue paint. Sometimes the upper rim is a natural wood color. The "pad" is a piece of sturdy cardboard decorated with various graphics that do not always match the paint of the play pen.

One of the carriages Effanbee offered for Dy-Dee was black with art-deco graphics, an oil-cloth hood and a pocket inside for the doll's bottle. Its heavy-duty springs and rubber tires ensured that Dy-Dee would have a smooth ride.

Vintage wicker doll carriages, such as this one, are also a wonderful way to display Dy-Dee dolls.

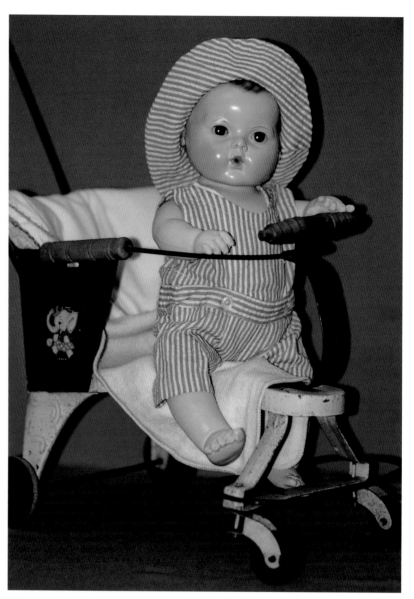

Dy-Dee from Mold 2 fits perfectly into this vintage doll Taylor-Tot. She wears her original Effanbee sun hat and romper.

her ride. These buggies came in many different colors, with contrasting designs woven into the sides of the carriage. The interior of the hood and basket part of the carriage were lined with fabric. These carriages also had strong spring mechanisms and large rubber-tired wheels for a smooth ride.

A popular staple of real baby equipment beginning in the late 1930s was the metal stroller, called a Taylor-Tot. This stroller had a wooden seat with a metal wrap-around chair-back. A metal tray fit under the baby's feet to keep them from dragging on the ground. While these useful pieces of baby-care essentials were not made expressly for Dy-Dee, they were undoubtedly frequently used with Dy-Dee dolls.

Obviously, a doll with such a well-documented need to be fed would have to own a high chair. Again, determining if there was one specific chair sold by Effanbee just for Dy-Dee is difficult. The major catalogs, such as Sears Roebuck and Montgomery Ward, usually followed their pages of baby-doll advertising with a page or two of accessory furniture. Unlike the Bathinette, advertisements for these other doll furniture items do not state they were made expressly by, or for, Effanbee or Dy-Dee.

Dy-Dee is all set for lunch in her red-and-white vinyl upholstered high chair, circa 1950.

A 20-inch Dy-Dee from Mold 2 enjoys a moment with her own book, *Dy-Dee Doll's Days*. She has light-brunette molded hair, brown eyes and very soft facial coloring. She wears all-original clothing made by Effanbee: a blue-and-white-striped flannel pajama set and a pink "eiderdown" hooded robe edged with blue machine embroidery.

CHAPTER FIVE

PUBLICATIONS & RELATED TOYS

O NE OF THE MOST EFFECTIVE METHODS devised by Effanbee for promoting Dy-Dee was the creation of various publications for little girls, which were also meant to influence their mothers' thinking. The first publication, sent to toy departments in stores, or mailed to members of the Patsy Doll Club, was a regular newsletter called *The Patsytown News*.

In 1934 *The Patsytown News*, Volume 1, Number 2, announced Dy-Dee's arrival with a banner headline: "EXTRA! NEW DY-DEE BABY ARRIVES!" The sub-headlines claimed that the "New Dy-Dee Baby is Almost Human" and the article noted that Dy-Dee could drink water from her own bottle or a spoon. Just in case the reader did not realize how remarkable this baby doll was, the text went on to explain:

"Never before has there been such a Wonder-Doll. Every little girl who has Dy-Dee will feel like a truly grown-up Mother. And what a busy little Mother she'll be. DY-DEE needs the same loving care and attention that any living, breathing baby does.

DY-DEE drinks pure water and loves it. She'll coo sweetly when she's finished her bottle, to tell her little mother what a good time she's just had.

The little mother of DY-DEE must be ever watchful for her almost-human baby's comfort and happiness. For, like any real infant, DY-DEE must never be allowed to be uncomfortably wet. Be gentle with Baby, and like a real grown Mother, bathe her, powder her, feed her and change her diapers when necessary.

Sir Stork is now busy delivering DY-DEES to your favorite shop.

On another page of this 1934 newsletter the illustration from the inside of the lid of Dy-Dee's box was reprinted. It featured a

The Patsytown News was an inspired way for Effanbee to keep their name and products in front of little girls and their mothers. The headlines created excitement and the photographs made Dy-Dee seem that much more real.

EFFANBEE

The Patsytown News

·········· *A Newspaper for Your Doll* ··········

| It's always Fair Weather When the Patsys get together | | Official Newspaper of the Patsy Doll Cl |

Vol. II, No. 2   *Published by* FLEISCHAKER & BAUM, *Makers of* EFFᴀɴBEE DOLLS, 45 Greene St., New York, N. Y.   Entire contents copy 1935, by Fleischaker

EXTRA—DY-DEE NOW HAS BABY SISTER

NEW "PATRICIA" SISTERS POPULAR EVERYWHERE

Have Slim, Shapely Figures Like Real 12-Year Old Little Girls

ALSO BEAUTIFUL EXPRESSIVE BIG BLUE EYES WITH REAL EYELASHES AND REAL HUMAN HAIR WIGS

Patricia, and her sisters, Patricia-Kin, Patricia Joan, Patricia Ann, Patricia Lou and Patricia Ruth, are real typical American Girls. They're really beautiful, and they fill a long-felt demand for a "grown-up sister" for the Patsys. No wonder thousands of little Doll Mothers all over the country want one of the Patricia Sisters for their Doll Families!

The Patricia's have the slim, strong bodies of healthy, happy 12-year old girls—instead of the chubby bodies of their younger sisters. They're just as cute — only more grown up. And when you pick up Patricia or one of her sisters — you'll have the thrill of your life! For their strong molded bodies—so like the bodies of young girls just going into their teens—are beautifully finished. They actually have the smooth, satin-like feel of real skin!

PATRICIA'S FACE IS BEAUTIFUL

She has such a wonderful smile! Her chin is beautifully shaped. She has large, expressive eyes, with long soft eyelashes. They're bright and sparkling, like any healthy young girl's, and they close tight shut when she sleeps.

NATURAL HAIR WIG WITH CURLS

To top off Patricia's pretty face, she has a real human hair wig, softly curled all around into a beautiful coiffure. Her hair can be combed or recurled when necessary. You can tie hair ribbons into Patricia's hair, if you like.

Yes—Patricia and her sisters are really beautiful dolls — and the Patsy Family and the other EFFᴀɴBEE Dolls are certainly proud of their new older sisters. Patricia's clothes are all the latest style, and can be washed time after time without fading as they are made of tubfast fabrics. They can be taken off and put on so easily. You can also have additional clothes, shoes and stockings for the Patricias which are especially tailored and made by EFFᴀɴBEE. They are guaranteed to fit perfectly.

SEE PATRICIA AND HER SISTERS SOON

If you haven't yet seen Patricia and her sisters, ask Mother to take you with her the next time she goes to your favorite store. You'll find all the Patricias in the Doll Department.

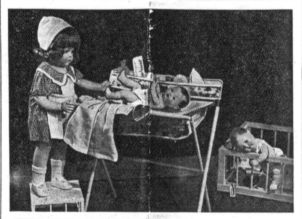

NURSE PATSY LOU IS ALWAYS BUSY taking care of Dy-Dee and her sisters. There's always something interesting for her to do, for the Dy-Dees need the same careful attention as real live babies. Here we see Nurse Patsy Lou getting ready to dress Dy-Dee after her bath, while Dy-Dee's sister in the play pen is trying to tell her that she has dropped her bottle.

NEW FAIRY PRINCESS DOLL DESIGNED BY COLLEEN MOORE — MADE BY EFFᴀɴBEE

Here's Patricia in Her New Sailor Coat, all ready to go off to a Patsy Picnic. Isn't she the healthy, happy little girl, though? Her coat is made of long-wearing blue serge, with a regular sailor collar—just the thing to wear during the Fall and Spring, and on the warmer winter days.

Miss Moore, Noted Moving Picture Star, Selected EFFᴀɴBEE To Make Fairy Princess Doll For Her

Miss Colleen Moore is widely known for her wonderful work in the moving pictures. But she's almost as well known for her large collection of Dolls from all over the world — and for her amazingly complete Doll House which she built for her dolls at a cost of almost half a million dollars. And when Miss Moore designed her now famous "Fairy Princess Doll,"—which is just the right size to live in her wonderful Doll House—she selected EFFᴀɴBEE to make it for her. Because, after seeing Dolls from all over the world, she felt that EFFᴀɴBEE Dolls were better made, better finished, more realistic and lifelike. You really should have at least two or more Fairy Princesses for your Doll Family.

Be sure to see "Fairy Princess" at your favorite Toy Department, and watch the newspapers and see when Miss Moore's wonderful Doll House is coming to your city. It's really worth seeing. For it is an exact miniature of a real Castle—complete with furniture and everything.

(Picture of Colleen Moore's Fairy Princess Doll is shown on Page 2.)

PATRICIA CONTEST PRIZE-WINNERS ON PAGE 4

CUTE LITTLE DY-DEE-ETTE IS NEW; ALMOST-HUMA DY-DEE BABY

Dy-Dee's New Sister Requir Same Care as Dy-Dee H

Special to *The* PATSYTOWN N
By Reporter PATSY LOU

Dy-Dee is all excited abo new Baby Sister, Dy-Dee-Ett fact, all Patsytown is thri know that Dy-Dee and her sister, Dy-Dee Lou now hav tle sister. As soon as I hea news, I rushed right over EFFᴀɴBEE Nursery to s new arrival.

I'm certainly glad I did—f Dee-Ette is just about the little baby I ever saw! She like Dy-Dee and Dy-Dee Lo smaller—only 11 inches tall. just love her, when you s sparkling eyes, her pert littl bud mouth, and her swee real-baby face. No wonder is proud of her. I don't bla one bit!

WHAT A BUSY TIME NURSE

When I called, Dy-Dee, Lou and their new sister, I Ette, were just having thei ing. They were all drinkin their bottles and you shoul heard their contented coo they drank.

Nurse certainly was a bu son, with three Dy-Dee Ba take care of. She said "They're certainly sweet, a keep me pretty busy. But they the cutest things?" I with her. "After I feed Nurse continued, "I put t bed for a short nap."

As all the Dy-Dee Babi finished their bottles by th Nurse put them under the for their nap. I watche drop off into slumberland, ai their pretty eyes tight shut

DY-DEES REQUIRE ATTENTION

Nurse and I talked a whil she said, "I'll see if any Babies need attention now. you know, all the Dy-Dee D just like real live babies. Y actually wet their diaper they have been fed, and of wet diapers must be chai once. And I watched while changed Dy-Dee and her sis a little while Nurse told m time for the Dy-Dee's bath

(Continued on page 2, cc

large image of a little girl caring for Dy-Dee and four smaller drawings of other activities to share with Dy-Dee. In the regular article entitled "What is New in the Shops," Aunt Patsy wrote, "Dy-Dee mothers can purchase a package of three Birdseye diapers and six safety pins, all neatly packed in cellophane and tied with a ribbon, for 25 cents." Available separately were bottles; booties; organdy dresses; silk coats; bathrobes; sleeping garments; sheets and pillows; as well as a ribbon-trimmed wool bunting made with a zipper, available in pink or blue. Effanbee also offered a three-piece knitted set, consisting of a sacque, cap and booties. An overnight case for travel with Dy-Dee included the doll and everything necessary to take the doll on a weekend trip: a supply of diapers; bottles; a clothes line; clothes pins; powder; soap; and a sponge.

In Volume 1, Number 3, *The Patsytown News* continued to enhance the image of Dy-Dee as an almost-real baby doll, under the front page headline: "EXTRA! DY-DEE CAPTURES MILLIONS OF HEARTS!" The sub-headlines stated that Dy-Dee Baby has cooed and won her way into hearts of everyone who sees her. The "star reporter" for the article was listed as Effanbee's own Miss Patsy Lou. She wrote:

When I arrived at the EFFanBEE Nursery, Dy-Dee was having her morning bottle. She lay in her little crib, with her pretty eyes open, smiling, eagerly drinking a bottle which she clasped in her diminutive hands. Fascinated, I watched bubbles rise in the bottle, and listened to her contented gurgling. Soon, Nurse took the bottle from her to give her a rest. But Dy-Dee lay there, with hands outstretched, cooing for more.

When Dy-Dee finished her bottle, Nurse fixed her pillows and made her comfortable. It was time for Dy-Dee's nap, but since I had come a long way to interview her, Nurse allowed her to stay up a little while.

I said, "Good morning, Dy-Dee and she answered, pleasantly, 'Coo.' Did you enjoy your bottle? And again, sweetly, she repeated 'Coo."

Dy-Dee looked sleepy, and I suggested to Nurse that if she could sit on my lap, it might keep her awake. Nurse agreed and placed Dy-Dee in my arms. 'Oh, Nurse,' I said, 'How soft and cuddly she feels! I just love her!'

'Everybody does,' answered Nurse, very much as if she knew

The Effanbee publications aimed to show little girls the many activities they could share with Dy-Dee, as well as to inform them about new dolls and new items available. Part of the appeal of *The Patsytown News* was that it often featured children and dolls engaged in activities girls would want to emulate.

DY-BEE BABY AT THE SEA SHORE   DY-DEE ALWAYS FLOATS

EVERYONE IS ENTERING THE CONTEST   MANY WILL WIN FINE PRIZES

DY-DEE SUN SONG
(TO THE TUNE OF BAA BAA BLACK SHEEP)

PATSY CLUB SONG
(TO THE TUNE OF REUBEN, REUBEN)

Imagine the fun of having a comic strip featuring your favorite doll. Many little Dy-Dee mothers undoubtedly learned to sing the Dy-Dee Sun Song, too.

this was no news to her. I looked at Dy-Dee as she lay there in my arms with her head slightly turned to the right. She had fallen asleep! I sat her up, but she slept so we put her back into her crib.

'Does she require much attention?' I whispered. Nurse replied, 'Why yes, Dy-Dee needs the same care and attention as a living, breathing human baby.' But how,' I asked, 'After all, she's only a doll.'

'Only a Doll?' Nurse seemed horrified at my expression. 'Would you like to spend the day with only a doll! Then you'll realize that Dy-Dee is more than just a doll; she's an almost-human baby!'

'Oh, may I?' I asked happily. 'I'd love to, and may I help take care of her?' Nurse smiled and said, 'Of course."

In charming articles such as these Effanbee helped create the illusion that their new Dy-Dee Baby was truly almost-human. In 1935 Effanbee continued to enhance Dy-Dee Baby's image as an almost-real baby. The front-page article in *The Patsytown News*, Volume 3, Number 1, discussed how Dy-Dee's "skin" feels just like a real baby's, that she is completely unbreakable and that she loves her bath. The special joints in her body prevent water from entering her body. In fact, Dy-Dee could go swimming with her little mother because her special joints allowed her to float in water! Among Dy-Dee's other talents: she could be taught to keep her eyes open when she is laid down, and to keep them closed even when she is held upright. To make Dy-Dee sleep, even if she is held upright, her head must be turned gently to the right while her eyes are closed. If the little mother turned Dy-Dee's head to the right while her eyes were open, she would not go to sleep, even if she were put down for a nap. Certainly no other doll could do that! The photograph accompanying this article showed two Dy-Dees in their sun-suits and sun hats, playing at the beach.

This 1935 newsletter also announced that Dy-Dee had just made a movie, which was to be shown in toy stores all over the county. It featured a typical busy day in the life of Dy-Dee. A comic strip called "Dy-Dee at the Sea Shore" was included in this issue, too. Finally, the issue closed with a charming little piece of music, to be sung to the tune of "Baa-baa Black Sheep," called "Dy-Dee Sun Song."

In Volume 2, Number 2, of the newsletter, the banner headline trumpeted the news that "DY-DEE NOW HAS A BABY SISTER!" Of course, the new baby sister required the very same attention and care as her big sister. The new Dy-Dee, named Dy-Dee-ette, was 11 inches long. This little doll, destined to remain popular for three decades, became the third in the Dy-Dee Family, joining the original 15-inch Dy-Dee and the second 20-inch doll. In 1938 a fourth doll, the 9-inch Dy-Dee-Wee, was introduced. The photo accompanying this article showed "Nurse" Patsy Lou (a beloved member of Effanbee's Patsy family of dolls) preparing Dy-Dee for her bath. Beside the Bathinette is a small playpen where Dy-Dee-ette is playing. The text of the story underlined that Dy-Dee and her sisters are not like "ordinary dolls. They're almost human and need the same loving care as real babies." The article went on to suggest: "You should really have all three of the Dy-Dees to start a Dy-Dee Family." Dy-Dee-ette was also offered as a premium for subscriptions in the December 1935 issue of *Junior Home*, a magazine for children. The doll offered was shown wearing a diaper and shirt and "holding" her bottle

The year 1936 was a busy one for Dy-Dee. Volume 3, Number 1, of *The Patsytown News* featured a front-page article by "A Little Effanbee Doll Mother," which told the story of her trip to the beach with Dy-Dee. The little author related how she spent days planning what clothes to take for Dy-Dee to wear. The list of items necessary for their visit included: "a sun-suit, extra diapers, extra bands and slips, one of her best bathrobes to wear in the house, and an older one to wear to the beach, a rubber lap sheet, talcum powder, absorbent cotton, and an extra pair of

DY-DEE SUN SUITS
EFFANBEE Tailored to Fit DY-DEE BABY

Effanbee encouraged Dy-Dee mothers to take their dolls to the beach. This allowed the children to play in the water with their dolls, underscoring Dy-Dee's almost-human qualities.

The small black-and-white book entitled *Dy-Dee Doll's Days* was published in 1938. On the cover, the doll seems to be inviting readers to come into her book and enjoy a day with her.

rubber panties. Of course, Dy-Dee needs all these things because she requires exactly the same care as a real baby." The reporter continued that she dressed Dy-Dee in her prettiest dress, added a pink sweater so she would not catch a cold and gathered several pillows to make Dy-Dee comfortable on the trip. Extra nursing bottles were also filled with "pure water" for the trip. (Some little doll mothers were apparently beginning to get creative when feeding Dy-Dee, for articles in the newsletter began to emphasize that Dy-Dee "should be fed only the purest water.")

In another article it was noted that "Dy-Dee Lou is a little larger than Dy-Dee, and Dy-Dee-ette is a little smaller." Yet in a separate article about the Effanbee Doll Family Reunion, author Patsy Lou wrote that "Next came Dy-Dee, Dy-Dee-ette, Dy-Dee-Kin and Dy-Dee Lou." This was the first mention of the fourth size of Dy-Dee. It was not until 1937 that the exact sizes of the Dy-Dee babies were listed in *The Patsytown News*: Dy-Dee is 15 inches (although earlier articles state she is 14½ inches); Dy-Dee-Kin is 13 inches; Dy-Dee-ette is 11 inches; and Dy-Dee-Wee is 9 inches. Dy-Dee Lou is the great big beautiful Dy-Dee measuring

The book was illustrated by black-and-white photos of Dy-Dee engaged in activities babies love, such as playing with a telephone.

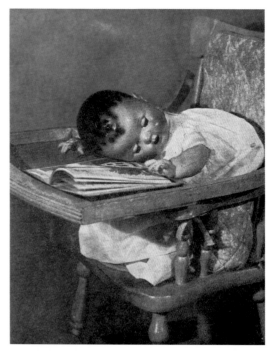

On another page, Dy-Dee is shown asleep over her book at dinner after a very busy day.

a full 20 inches length. (Helpfully, the Dy-Dee babies' names tell us immediately which size they are.)

In *The Patsytown News*, Volume 4, Number 2, Dy-Dee again had the banner headline: "DY-DEE IS THE DOLL I WANT!" The writers at Effanbee went on to state that, "Santa Claus is getting thousands of letters about Dy-Dee." In one picture, Dy-Dee was shown for the first time as a tousle head with a caracul wig that the doll mothers could shampoo and comb. The dolls were available with either molded hair or the new wigs. Also introduced in this issue was the official Dy-Dee Baby Coach, an elegant carriage made by a leading manufacturer of carriages for real infants. The carriage had rubber tires, easy-riding springs, and special pockets for Dy-Dee's bottle, powder, and extra diapers. The new layettes pictured in black-and-white drawings included such items as a zippered bunting with attached hat, a boxed set with a dress, kimono, blanket, three bottles, a hot water bottle, diapers and other goodies—all packaged in a special Dy-Dee box with unique graphics. Other boxed sets included simple or fancy dresses and underwear, or elaborate christening gowns and matching coats of embroidered silk. Finally, Effanbee promoted their doctor and nurse sets to keep Dy-Dee well. "The Patsy Doctor Outfit has a real Doctor's uniform for Brother to wear to be the Doctor. The Patsy Nurse outfit has a real Nurse's uniform." (Obviously, this announcement was made at a time when it was assumed boys would be doctors and girls would be their nurses!)

In a special report on the Effanbee Christmas Party, "Patricia" wrote, "The Dy-Dees were all wheeled into the party in their beautiful new Dy-Dee Coaches. All the little nurses wore Patsy Nurse Uniforms. The Dy-Dees were all presented with wonderful new layettes with extra dresses, caps, bonnets, warm buntings and slippers. After the dinner, the Dy-Dee Nurses fed the Dy-Dee Babies their pure water out of their bottles and the Dy-Dee

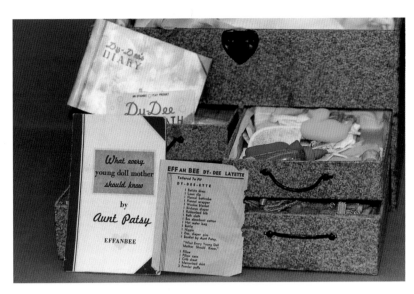

This trunk filled with Dy-Dee goodies belongs to a 20-inch Dy-Dee Lou. It includes her Dy-Dee Diary and the booklet by Aunt Patsy entitled "What Every Young Doll Mother Should Know," as well as an inventory of her layette and her very own bubble bath.

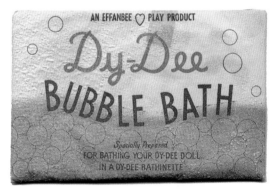

Bubble bath, personalized for Dy-Dee's use, was often included in the layette sets. This is a close view of the package in the set shown above.

AUNT PATSY
NEW YORK

Dear Little Doll Mother,
Now that you are the mother of such a truly human doll as Dy-Dee Baby, I feel that I can talk to you just as I would to a real grown-up mother.

The pamphlet includes a message to the doll mother from Aunt Patsy, which begins: "Now that you are the mother of such a truly human doll as Dy-Dee Baby, I feel that I can talk to you just as I would to a real grown-up mother." These words must have delighted young girls who wanted to feel like grown-up mothers.

dolls, tired out by all the excitement, dropped off to sleep."

Another favorite publication commissioned by Effanbee was a little hard-cover book: *Dy-Dee Doll's Days*, written by Peggy Vandegriff, photographed by Lawson Fields and published by Rand McNally & Company. The book was introduced in 1938. The delightful black-and-white photographs detailed the activities of a Dy-Dee mother's day. Pictures captured a sweet little girl going about her duties as the mother of Dy-Dee. Full-page photographs depicted Dy-Dee drinking her bottle; being weighed; reading her daily schedule; having her bath in an enamelware tub; being powdered after the bath; being rocked to sleep; and asleep in her crib. They also showed the little girl drawing a portrait of Dy-Dee, bandaging Dy-Dee's hands to prevent her from sucking her thumb and taking Dy-Dee for a walk in her carriage. In addition, Dy-Dee visited a school classroom; stood up in her playpen; played in the sandbox; hung out her laundry; played in the backyard sprinkler; and finally, collapsed and slept while waiting for her dinner in the highchair.

Other publications that enhanced the play value of the Dy-Dee dolls were the instruction books included with Dy-Dee purchases, such as "How to Play with a Doll." One favorite is the fold-out booklet called "What Every Young Doll Mother Should Know" by Aunt Patsy. The cover is ivory with blue and pink edges. This little guide shows how to care for Dy-Dee baby, while also showing all the clever things Dy-Dee can do. Each new version of this little booklet contained some of the old graphics, but also included updated images. One of the first booklets to include an actual photograph of Dy-Dee was published in 1949, when the doll acquired new holes along her upper nose that allowed her to "cry." The photograph also showed Dy-Dee in her caracul wig. (Earlier graphics showed Dy-Dee with painted hair.)

Another doll that Effanbee introduced captured the headlines in *The Patsytown News*, Volume 4, Number 2, in 1937. A large photograph showed Charlie McCarthy, accompanied by

BATHING

When you bathe your baby, hold her head above the water, although water will not hurt her head. You may use pure soap and plenty of water. Although Dy-Dee has movable arms, legs and head, her body may safely be submerged in water. Her air-tight joints will not permit the water to enter her body.

CLEANING EARS WITH Q-TIPS

Your new DyDee Doll has adorable soft flexible ears. So we suggest that you use a Q-Tip and gently clean her dainty ears at least once a day. Use soap and water and clean Dy-Dee's ears very thoroughly. Then dry and powder.

BLOWING BUBBLES

You can have lots of fun making DY-DEE blow soap bubbles. It is so simple! Just dip the bubble pipe bowl in soapy suds, place the nippled stem in DY-DEE'S mouth. Now press DY-DEE'S tummy gently and slowly. My, what beautiful soap bubbles DY-DEE blows!

A later version of the pamphlet included more color and used photographs of Dy-Dee in addition to illustrations.

his ventriloquist partner, Edgar Bergen, making their first visit to Patsytown. Effanbee used the occasion to announce that Charlie was now a member of the Effanbee Family of dolls. Charlie admitted in a headline that "he thought babies were a bother until he visited the Dy-Dee Nursery." The story introducing Charlie McCarthy focused on his reaction to all the clever things Dy-Dee could do, rather than on the doll herself.

In this issue, a special information box announced that "Dy-Dee now drinks from a spoon and just loves it!" The inside pages of this newsletter were devoted to five large photographs (supposedly taken by Charlie McCarthy himself!) of little girls in nurse's costumes, caring for Dy-Dee dolls, including one of Dy-Dee drinking water from her spoon while sitting up. Another photograph showed Dy-Dee enjoying her bath in her "real" Bathinette. (The fact that Dy-Dee can float in her bath was

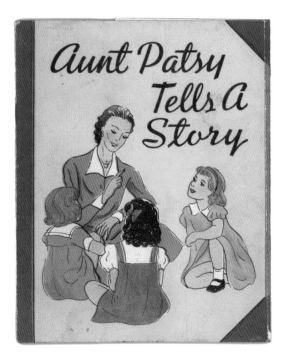

In 1938 Patsy Doll Club members received a small storybook created by Effanbee entitled *Aunt Patsy Tells a Story*.

The colorful illustrations inside the book depict Aunt Patsy teaching a little girl named Barbara how to tend to her Dy-Dee.

mentioned.) Yet another picture showed Dy-Dee prepared to nap in her carriage, while her little mother sat nearby reading *Aunt Patsy Tells a Story*. In a separate article readers learned that they could receive their own free copy of the new book, *Aunt Patsy Tells a Story*, at their favorite toy shop, or by writing to Aunt Patsy at Effanbee Doll Company.

The beautiful Dy-Dee Diary, another popular booklet from Effanbee, was also discussed in the newsletter. Little girls were encouraged to keep track of all the fun they were having with their Dy-Dee dolls. The Diary had pages for friends to write what they thought of Dy-Dee, as well as pages to tell all about her arrival, gifts, trips, games and layette items.

The back page of this issue of the newsletter featured two new items that were made available just in time for Christmas. The first was a new layette for Dy-Dee, extolled as a "Beautiful and Useful Christmas Present." This boxed set, with the familiar Dy-Dee graphics in the lid, was only one of "hundreds of layettes for Dy-Dee which you will see at your favorite toy store." The other new item was a complete outfit for Dy-Dee mothers, beautifully boxed with a new graphic design in its lid. The set included a "nicely fitting lawn uniform and cap, a rubber apron to protect little mother's clothes when bathing Dy-Dee, an extra nursing bottle, talcum, cotton, a powder puff, and a cute little wash cloth." In addition there was a water bottle and the new Dy-Dee Diary.

Another Effanbee publication mailed to the Patsy Doll Club members in 1938 was the brightly colored little storybook titled *Aunt Patsy Tells a Story*. The little book (5 inches x 6 ½ inches) was illustrated on each page with colorful drawings depicting a little girl named Barbara, searching for a "baby doll as beautiful as my new baby sister." Of course, the kindly Aunt Patsy is happy to help little Barbara with her search. Aunt Patsy seeks inspiration in a hospital newborn nursery, in parks where mothers bring their babies for fresh air and at the baby parade in Atlantic City. As Aunt Patsy tells us, "After my trip, I set to work and soon had the most wonderful baby doll imaginable…Dy-Dee Baby!" Aunt Patsy decides to save this wonderful surprise for Barbara's

Queen Holden appears to have painted her Dy-Dee paper doll directly from an actual doll, surrounding it with baby toys and care products. She even included a little baby book for recording Dy-Dee's story. (This cut paper doll is from the collection of Jean Sullivan.)

Queen Holden perfected a technique to give the paper doll sleep-eyes. With the special eye-piece in place, Dy-Dee is ready for her nap.

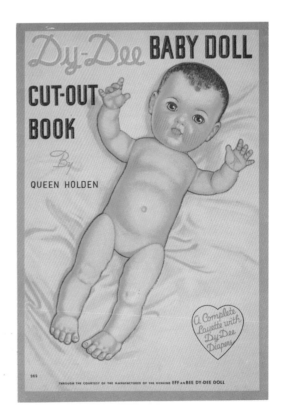

The *Dy-Dee Baby Doll Cut-Out Book* was a collaboration of Effanbee with the Whitman Publishing Company in 1938. The artist, Queen Holden, had been creating best-selling paper dolls for Whitman for nine years by then.

birthday and goes on to tell the reader that she "can hardly tell you how thrilled Barbara was, how she hugged and kissed both me and Dy-Dee Baby. I have never seen such joy!" Early the next day, Aunt Patsy returns to Barbara's house to show her how to care for her Dy-Dee doll. In the course of teaching Barbara how to care for Dy-Dee, Aunt Patsy is able to extol all the unique features of this "almost-real" baby doll.

Another successful promotional piece for Effanbee was *My Doll's Magazine*, which contained realistic articles, advertisements, and "teasers" about new products that would soon be introduced by Effanbee—all supposedly written by the friendly Miss Patsy. And for the parents who might be confused about the

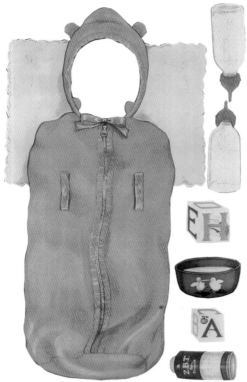

In the paper-doll set, the bunting for Dy-Dee was cleverly designed to include her little scalloped pillow.

One of the costumes included was a blue-and-white dotted-Swiss dress with lace-edged bib yoke and the popular butterfly sleeves. A bonnet and a blue gingham romper were also included. Even the shoes and socks were carefully drawn.

right doll to purchase for their daughters, Effanbee helpfully offered a booklet entitled "How to Select the Proper Doll to Suit Your Child's Age."

In a remarkable example of two businesses co-operating, the Whitman Publishing Company produced a highly desirable *Dy-Dee Baby Doll Cut-Out Book* in collaboration with the Effanbee Doll Company in 1938. The artist selected for this project was Queen Holden, who had been creating best-selling paper dolls for Whitman for nine years. Holden was known for her beautifully soft and life-like renderings of babies and children. The paper-doll book included a 14-inch doll and her layette, complete with toys, dishes, powder, a Bathinette and clothing drawn from Dy-Dee's actual layette items. The set even had a "real" textured paper diaper. ("This gimmicky diaper was totally impractical. Once the diaper was put on the paper Dy-Dee, her other clothing would not lay down properly," says Loraine Burdick, paper doll historian and publisher of *Celebrity Doll Journal*.)

The paper-doll clothing so accurately depicted actual layette items found in Dy-Dee layettes that one can assume Queen Holden painted her version of Dy-Dee directly from an actual doll and her clothing. On a page with alphabet blocks and a blue feeding bowl, the artist drew a white bonnet, blue dotted-Swiss dress with embroidered white collar and a blue gingham romper to go under the dress. Other toys included with the paper doll Dy-Dee were a pink-and-white roly-poly doll, a pink ball rattle and a spin-around musical rattle. In addition, there was a warm pink romper with four tiny tucks on each shoulder and an embroidered white organdy collar. At the bottom of the page, a note cautioned: "The special tissue paper in the book is to be used for diapers for the Dy-Dee doll. Mother will show you how to cut the tissue to make the diapers and she will also show you how to put them on your doll."

Another page featured a plain blue slip, white undershirt,

white socks and shoes and a charming blue dotted-Swiss dress and bonnet. The first page in the paper-doll book depicted a pink silk coat and hat, as well as pink rubber panties. Other items on the page were a can of ZBT baby powder and Johnson & Johnson cotton. These other companies undoubtedly welcomed this exposure to a generation of future little mothers. This page also had several rattles and Dy-Dee's own curved-handle spoon.

The final page of the book helped get Dy-Dee ready for an outing with a zipper-fronted bunting, carriage pillow and two nursing bottles. A particularly nice touch was the little baby book that the doll mother could fill in to share her Dy-Dee paper doll baby's story.

The back cover featured a Bathinette and a hot water bottle, as well as a rather strange-looking item, meant to be cut out and used to allow the paper Dy-Dee baby to close her eyes. Queen Holden had perfected a technique whereby a small slit could be made above each eye, and an additional piece, with thick eyelashes, could be pushed through the slits to cover the eyes. Effanbee's emphasis on realism for Dy-Dee obviously extended even to this paper doll!

In another alliance, Effanbee commissioned a set of jigsaw puzzles, featuring various Effanbee dolls. One of the puzzles showed Dy-Dee enjoying her bath in her specially-made Bathinette. She was being bathed by a large Effanbee doll dressed in a blue-and-white striped uniform with a white apron and starched nurse's cap. In the background, Dy-Dee's clean laundry—including her pajamas, a diaper and an undershirt—is hanging out to dry. Other puzzles in the set depicted Effanbee dolls contemporary to this Mold 2 Dy-Dee from 1940.

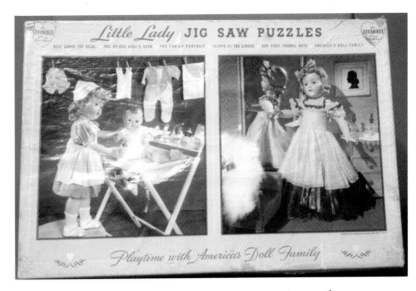

Effanbee also commissioned a set of jigsaw puzzles featuring their various dolls, including Dy-Dee. This circa-1940 set has six different puzzles depicting different Effanbee dolls.

Dy-Dee is enjoying her bath in the puzzle that features this doll.

The blue coat and hat set, made in sturdy cotton file, is one of Dy-Dee's most recognizable layette sets. The white cotton loop trim on the coat and hat was sometimes referred to as "lace" in Effanbee advertisements. It is modeled here by a 15-inch Dy-Dee from Mold 3.

CHAPTER SIX

PUBLICITY & ADVERTISING

THE MARKETING GENIUS of the founders of Effanbee Doll Company, especially Hugo Baum, who delighted in being known as the "Ziegfield of the doll world," was undoubtedly one reason for the success and longevity of this company. Effanbee promoted Dy-Dee through a multi-faceted marketing approach. The doll was available through mail-order catalogs, as well as in toy sections of department stores and eventually, luxury editions of Dy-Dee and her layettes and accessories were produced for high-end stores, such as FAO Schwarz. Dy-Dee was marketed heavily to the toy industry, as well as in the general press. The many "photo opportunities" staged by Effanbee also enhanced the appeal of Dy-Dee. A very extensive advertising campaign, both in trade journals and in national consumer magazines, constantly reminded girls and their mothers that this baby doll was unlike any earlier doll.

Beyond traditional advertising and publicity, however, the company also arranged parties for little girls in the leading department stores in large cities, formed Effanbee doll clubs for girls by mail, and published or commissioned booklets, story books, a paper doll and jigsaw puzzles (see chapter five). The company also offered incentives for children to "earn" Effanbee dolls or informational materials. Effanbee hired women to portray the mythical "Aunt Patsy," who supposedly wrote all the charming booklets for the proud owners of Dy-Dee babies and other Effanbee dolls. Aunt Patsy was also the

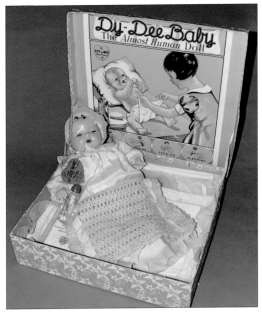

In a luxurious set made by Effanbee exclusively for FAO Schwarz a Dy-Dee from Mold 1 was presented in a ribbon-trimmed crocheted blanket.

Effanbee often used the same graphics in two or three slightly different ads in the same magazine. This ad is from the November 1947 issue of *Children's Activities*.

Another Effanbee ad from 1947 depicts the same little girl, dressed as a nurse, caring for her Dy-Dee.

name given to the women Effanbee hired to present seminars on doll care in department stores and toy shops around the country. These Aunt Patsy actresses wore nurses' white uniforms and demonstrated how to care for Effanbee dolls, using a full range of Effanbee products. These doll events were enormously popular and well-attended.

While Effanbee tirelessly promoted their entire doll line, they reserved the most intense and long-lasting campaign for Dy-Dee Baby. The well-known Effanbee researcher Patricia Schoomaker says, "Dy-Dee is a researcher's dream; I doubt any other doll was so heavily advertised." The owners of Effanbee must have realized that this doll was so revolutionary in concept that she had to be seen to be believed. The advertising and publicity campaign they created for the introduction of Dy-Dee was a model for saturation product advertising.

Dy-Dee baby was first mentioned in 1933, but the advertising "blitz" did not begin until *Playthings* magazine's September 1934 issue. Dy-Dee was shown wearing a long white dress and reclining on a ruffled pillow, while drinking her bottle, which is held by her child "mother." The ad explained that Dy-Dee could drink from her bottle, and that her new mother should then be mindful to watch for a wet diaper. In addition to this realistic behavior, Dy-Dee could be safely bathed because her joints were water-tight, preventing the bath water from entering her body. For this same reason, Dy-Dee could actually float in her bath or at the sea-shore. Other rubber dolls of that time could be placed in a tub of water, but their bodies quickly filled with water which then was very difficult to drain out of their bodies. Dy-Dee has unique sealed joints so that the water entering her body can

This colorful undated offer was published as part of a magazine promotion for Popsicles, a frozen treat.

only come through "drinking" her bottle.

The initial advertising was quite successful: Effanbee sold more than 25,000 Dy-Dee dolls the first year of production—a real marketing coup. In 1936 more than 750,000 Dy-Dee dolls were sold!

Effanbee used both photography and illustrations to depict Dy-Dee in catalogs and magazines. Effanbee often used images from one advertisement to enhance another ad as well. In addition to ads for Dy-Dee aimed at children and often published in children's magazines, Effanbee also ran black-and-white ads directed to the mothers of little girls. One advertisement read, in part:

> "This life-like EFFanBEE doll is the nearest thing to a real baby! Dy-Dee can drink from a bottle or spoon, blow soap bubbles and sleep sitting up, or lie awake. She even needs to be watched for diaper changes, since she is no different than an ordinary baby after a big glass of water. Dy-Dee is so well constructed and jointed that your child can give her baby daily baths, washing the baby's satin-smooth skin and soft flexible rubber ears, without worrying about getting water into the body and destroying it. This realness gives your daughter valuable training in handling real babies by dressing, bathing, feeding and handling and caring for her Dy-Dee. Dy-Dee has a wardrobe any baby would be proud to own."

On October 30, 1947, Effanbee placed colorful half-page ads in various Sunday comics sections of large city newspapers, which included a coupon for a sixteen-page Effanbee catalog. A child could receive the catalog by filling in the coupon and including five cents in coins or stamps. This ad showed the little child mother in her Effanbee-made

Effanbee placed this ad for Dy-Dee in a 1950 issue of the trade magazine *Toys and Novelties.*

The 1937 article in *Life* magazine about Dy-Dee dolls was a major publicity coup for the Effanbee Doll Company. The opening page of the story showed a little girl spending the day with her Dy-Dee.

750,000 DY-DEE DOLLS GRATIFY THE MATERNAL INSTINCT OF MODERN YOUNGSTERS

Feeding. After you squeeze the air out of her stomach, Dy-Dee will suck in water either from a bottle or spoon.

DY-DEE BABY IS DEDICATED TO "EVERY LITTLE GIRL WHO HAS THE CAPACITY FOR MOTHER LOVE"

Washing. Dy-Dee's soft-rubber body is air and watertight and can therefore be bathed despite her movable limbs.

Dressing. Dy-Dee layettes come in trunks, include such essentials as rubber panties, diapers, bottles and nipples.

Promenading. In a $35 doll carriage with collapsible top, this little New Yorker airs her $28 infant. Note the rattle.

In an old, rambling, six-story, brick building on Greene Street, New York City, heavy-muscled men and nimble-fingered girls are working overtime to fill the rush of Christmas orders for that phenomenon of the toy world—the Dy-Dee doll who wets her diapers. Now four years old, Dy-Dee is, more than ever, the most popular doll in the world.

When functional Dy-Dee was introduced in 1933, her behavior was so unconventional that only the most broad-minded mammas or prankish bachelor uncles thought her a suitable plaything for innocent youngsters. On her first trip to England, she was promptly ejected from Harrod's in London. Not until the Duchess of Kent, shortly after, asked for and got one, was Dy-Dee put on display.

Regardless of what prudish grownups may think, Dy-Dee sales prove that she is a little girl's dream of a doll come true. By this Christmas, her makers (Fleischaker and Baum; trade name Effanbee) estimate that 750,000 Dy-Dees will have reached the laps of the little mothers of the world. They range in price from $3 to $28, depending on size and wardrobe. The doll and complete equipment with which the little girl plays on these pages costs $100.

CONTINUED ON NEXT PAGE

nurse's costume, and included drawings of Dy-Dee's layette, the Dy-Dee Nursing Set and the Bathinette, made especially for Dy-Dee. A black-and-white version of this ad was also placed in the October 1947 issue of *Children's Activities* magazine. In 1950 Effanbee, by then owned by Noma Electric Company, created a

Dy-Dee Doll (continued)

1 Fifteen minutes after feeding, Dy-Dee automatically wets her diaper. After removing rubber pants, Joanna tackles the job of diaper-changing.

2 Powdering is the next step. Instruction books warn to powder carefully so doll will be "fresh, clean, and sweet as a daisy." Milk should never be fed to Dy-Dees, as it curdles in the inner tube, producing a lasting rancid smell.

3 Properly fitting the clean diaper is hard work for her inexperienced hands.

4 Pinning on the diaper. In some State health departments, Dy-Dees are used to teach infant care to nurses and expectant mothers.

CONTINUED ON PAGE 58

Dy-Dee Doll (continued)

From 1,500 to 2,000 Dy-Dee dolls are now being turned out daily in the Fleischaker & Baum factory in New York City. The bodies of soft rubber, and the heads of hard rubber, are made in Akron, by the Miller Rubber Co., Inc. The assembling, finishing and dressing are done in New York.

Above is a rack of finished heads for the $3 to $8.50 dolls. These have no wigs. The curls, as well as the lashes, eyebrows and lips, are hand-painted. The flesh tints of head are sprayed on with an airbrush. A diabolical machine with two steel plungers gouges eye sockets. A similar machine with one plunger makes the mouth cavity.

Below is a stack of dolls ready to be dressed. These have washable "skin wigs," swathed in tissue paper for protection against handling. Every doll is washed with soap and water before dressing. Number of undergarments depends on price of doll.

color ad that ran in several different publications. The colorful image showed a little girl preparing to bathe Dy-Dee beside the Christmas tree, which was hung with colorful balls, all of which showed a child caring for *her* Dy-Dee.

In December 1936, just in time for Christmas, *Fortune* magazine

The Montgomery Ward catalog for Christmas 1948 featured Dy-Dee in a half-page picture with her layette, and a much smaller image of another Effanbee baby, Sweetie Pie, in the lower right-hand corner.

These Mold 2 Dy-Dees make a pretty picture in a Christmas catalog from Montgomery Ward. In the lower corner is an example of "complementary advertising." The Amsco sterilizer set and the doll diaper bag are both appropriate for Dy-Dee, but they were not offered by Effanbee.

published the article entitled "Dolls—Made in America," which focused attention on the uniquely successful Effanbee Doll Company and their lead doll designer, Bernard Lipfert (see chapter one). The article was primarily interested in showing the strengths—and weaknesses—of the doll manufacturing business in America. The labor-intensive production process and the impact of labor unions on doll manufacturing were suitable subjects for this business magazine written for management-level readers and brought Effanbee to the attention of a new audience.

Dy-Dee dolls were advertised in Montgomery Ward catalogs for many years. This is an early ad from 1941.

The company worked very hard to get the Dy-Dee doll in front of the public. One of their real coups came when the November 1937 issue of *Life* magazine included an article about Dy-Dee, accompanied by eleven photographs showing a little girl caring for Dy-Dee throughout a busy day, plus two photographs of the manufacturing process. The article stated: "Now four years old, Dy-Dee is more than ever, the most popular doll in the world......Regardless of what prudish grownups may think, Dy-Dee sales prove that she is a little girl's dream of a doll come true." Effanbee had already announced that by Christmas 1937, "more than 750,000 Dy-Dee dolls would have reached the laps of little mothers all over the world." The article informed readers that Dy-Dee dolls range in price from three to twenty-eight dollars, depending on the size of the doll and her layette. If a little girl was fortunate enough to own all the accessories shown in the photographs which accompanied this article, the total price would be one hundred dollars! Dy-Dee was also shown in various other magazines in articles aiming to show parents what their children most wanted for Christmas.

The year 1939 saw another big publicity coup for Effanbee. Dy-Dee was given the keys to the New York World's Fair in a special ceremony at the Lagoon of Nations. By 1968 Effanbee was able to use the Dy-Dee doll name to introduce a whole new generation of little girls to Dy-Dee babies. An ad that year touted Effanbee—"For 59 years, the leader in quality dolls," with the opening headline: "Like Grandma and Mommy—now, her loveliest dreams come true...with Dy-Dee Darlin' by Effanbee!!!" The all-vinyl Dy-Dee Darlin' probably came closest to duplicating the most appealing qualities of the original Dy-Dee dolls, but even this doll did not capture the original charm (or market) that Dy-Dee did when first introduced.

Effanbee introduced Dy-Dee Darlin' in 1968 with a campaign directed at the childhood memories of women who were now mothers and grandmothers.

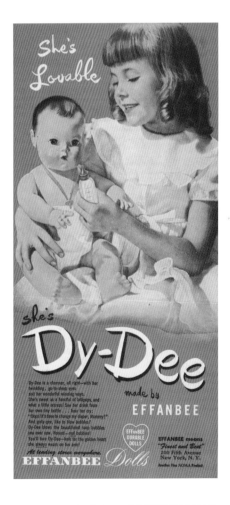

In 1948 this ad on a bright red background was printed in *Children's Activities*. The same ad was used repeatedly in this magazine, sometimes in black-and-white.

CHAPTER SEVEN

OTHER DRINK-AND-WET DOLLS

D UE TO THE ENORMOUS SUCCESS OF THE DY-DEE BABY, early in the doll's production imitations began to come on the market. In response, in a full-page advertisement in *Playthings'* May 1937 issue, Fleischaker & Baum took on the issue of commercial piracy. Effanbee announced that they had had to resort to law courts for protection, and that the courts had granted an injunctive relief against the wrongdoers. The court's ruling stated that the wrongdoers were: "permanently enjoined from manufacturing or selling, or offering to manufacture or sell, or filling orders for the manufacture or sale of a doll which, excepting functional features, in any way simulates or tends to simulate plaintiff's Dy-Dee doll."

The court went on to prohibit the use of "any statement, expression or slogan calculated or tending to create the impression that the doll being advertised is the Dy-Dee doll manufactured by plaintiffs***or any pictorial illustration of a girl feeding, nursing, or diapering a baby similar to those now used by plaintiffs." Fleischaker and Baum wrote that even though they "appreciate that imitation is the sincerest form of flattery, we, however, intend to protect our products and our rights.... from any other manufacturer who offers for sale a doll simulating our Dy-Dee doll." In the lower right-hand corner of the ad was a picture of Dy-Dee in her sun-suit at the beach.

The primary offender in the lawsuit brought by Effanbee was the American Character Doll Company, which had intro-

Fleischaker and Baum hoped to limit the damage done by other dollmakers who tried to copy their Dy-Dee baby doll. They published this ad prohibiting imitations in the trade journal *Playthings* in 1937.

Ideal created a charming drink-and-wet doll they named Betsy Wetsy in 1937. This green-eyed doll has a red caracul wig and holds an instruction sheet entitled, "To My New Mother, From: Betsy Wetsy." This 13-inch Betsy is wearing her original dress, bonnet and booties in pristine condition. The dress remains crisp and the embossing is intact because the dress has never been laundered. Bety Wetsy was discontinued in mid-1950. (Courtesy Kate Gellin)

duced a baby doll they called "Wee-Wee" in 1934. They were forced by this court action to rename their baby, and then marketed it as "Bottle-Tot." Other imitators included "Sunbabe" and "So-Wee," which were made by Sun Rubber Company. These dolls came in a suitcase with a layette and nursing bottles.

Ideal Toy and Novelty Company introduced their imitation, Betsy Wetsy, in 1937. The original Betsy is eleven inches high, with a hard-rubber head and painted hair. She has sleep eyes and a soft-rubber body. Eventually, Betsy Wetsy was made in a variety of sizes. The later dolls have hard-plastic heads and vinyl bodies.

Layettes were also available for Betsy Wetsy. There were even colorful graphics on the inside of the lid of the Betsy Wetsy layette cases. Ideal marketed their Betsy Wetsy at a lower price than the Dy-Dee, which meant not only that less was included in the layettes, but also that the quality, fine materials and artwork that were the hallmark of the Effanbee dolls were not a part of these sets. Nevertheless, Betsy Wetsy was an extremely popular doll and has many devoted fans among collectors today.

That same year, 1937-38, Ideal also introduced another imitation of Dy-Dee, Ducky Baby. However, Effanbee did not

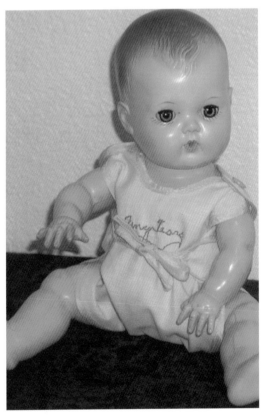

Tiny Tears came in a sweet romper with her name embroidered on it in red. This 11-inch doll has molded hair and a rubber body. (Courtesy Kate Gellin)

American Character Doll Company placed advertisements for Tiny Tears that were very similar in lay-out to the Effanbee ads for Dy-Dee. The ads for Tiny Tears showed more close-ups of the doll's head in order to provide a good view of the "tears" running down her face.

pursue legal action against Ideal for either doll. We can only surmise that Effanbee believed further legal action would be costly and impractical. Later, in 1950, American Character introduced their most successful imitation of Dy-Dee: the Tiny Tears doll, which "cried actual tears." She was available in four sizes: 12 inches, 13 inches, 15 inches and 18 ½ inches, with a vinyl body and a hard-plastic head with painted, caracul or rooted Saran hair. She came with layettes and other baby accessories.

Tiny Tears enjoyed a tie-in with the *Ding Dong* television show, which was very popular in the early 1950s. The Tiny Tears dolls were also advertised in 1958 in the Continental Products catalog, and the General Merchandise catalog. The doll remains popular with collectors today; one of the most difficult to find is the baby with the blonde caracul wig. A mint-in-box layette set with all of the pieces in place and unused can sell for more than nine hundred dollars today.

In the late 1940s and early 1950s, Sears Roebuck also sold their own imitation of Dy-Dee, called the "Happi-Time" Drinking-wetting Baby, with a layette and carrying case.

CHAPTER EIGHT

CLEANING & PRESERVING DY-DEE

EOPLE WHO LOVE the original Dy-Dee baby dolls face the problem of preserving these wonderful old rubber babies from the natural deterioration that occurs over time. (The newer vinyl Dy-Dee dolls require a different approach because they are made of vinyl, which is a chemical-based material.) These darling rubber babies were the ultimate play doll in the past, but their bodies are now tender with age and a vintage Dy-Dee is no longer suitable for child's play. The dolls we have today have passed from play-dolls to treasured artifacts. With gentle care, they will become the heirlooms of tomorrow.

The rubber used for the early Dy-Dee dolls is a natural substance made from the gum of the rubber tree. It is not "magic skin," vinyl, nor soft plastic—all words you will find used to describe Dy-Dee bodies. The hard rubber used for the heads and the softer rubber used for Dy-Dee's body are both made from natural rubber—the difference in texture is caused during the processing of the gum.

The first step is preserving any doll is to clean her. A basic doll-cleaning kit should include soft clean cloths and towels, mild liquid soap, a very soft toothbrush for getting into creases, a soft artist's paint brush for cleaning delicate areas around the eyes and nose, Q-tips and a great deal of patience!

Begin by washing your vintage Dy-Dee with warm soap and water. You may safely put Dy-Dee in a bowl of water if her joints are still squeaky tight and she has no open cracks. (If she has any breaks or cracks in her rubber, you should give her a sponge

Even Peggy Montei's cat, top right, could not believe the condition of this Dy-Dee as she was being removed from her cardboard shipping box. The doll was in an advanced stage of deterioration and her clothing was dirtier than she was. Given the over-all condition of this baby, it is amazing that her face remained pretty and undamaged. We can only surmise that the unique "seasoning" process for making the hard-rubber heads helped keep the face fresh.

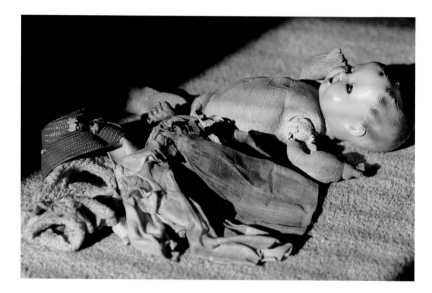

The extent of decay in the doll's arms became apparent when her clothing was removed for laundering.

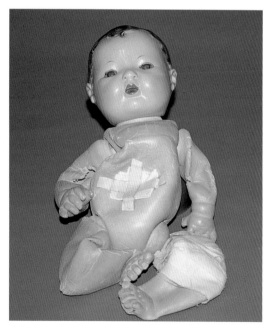

When the doll was completely undressed, it became clear that she had obviously been dearly loved by someone who tried to bandage up her "hurts."

bath rather than placing the entire doll in a tub of water.) You can tell if the mushroom joints are still water-tight if you can actually hear the squeaking of rubber on rubber when you move the doll's arms and legs. If you can hear the squeaking that ensures the joints are still sealed, you may safely place Dy-Dee in a tub of water—being certain to keep her eyes above water level, of course. Be sure to let her dry completely.

Never use any product that is greasy or has a petroleum base to it. You will find the ingredients listed on the cleaning product; if not, do not use that product on a doll. Read the labels and be sure it says the product is good for rubber. But be sure you do not use any product that states it is good for cleaning vinyl. Repairs past the step of thorough cleaning are best left to people who are trained to restore dolls and/or artifacts of similar materials.

The pictures in this book, except for the mint-in-case dolls, show Dy-Dee babies that needed cleaning and some amount of refurbishing. Their clothing also required hours of slow cleaning. The restoration of the dolls in this book has been done by the skilled and gentle hands of Peggy Montei. Her motto is: First, do no harm. Over the years, Peggy has become skilled at making the unique joints Dy-Dee requires and has taught herself the techniques necessary to recover these old natural rubber bodies. She is happy when she can recover even a few of these dolls.

While Peggy is not a professional restorer she believes it is important for Dy-Dee collectors to see what can be done; first with soap and water, and then with more complex techniques. If a doll needs further work, she suggests contacting professional doll repair artists to see if they are trained to work on natural rubber dolls.

More advice is provided by Nicholas J. Hill, author of *The Definitive Book on the Care and Preservation of Vinyl Dolls and Action Figures* (Twin Pines Press, 2000). A formulating organic chemist who holds patents in plastics technology, he brings a very scientific approach to the preservation and cleaning of dolls. Nicholas is writing a second book that details how to preserve and clean dolls of all materials. He has generously shared the following suggestions for care of Dy-Dee dolls.

Today's rubber is not what it used to be. What we know as rubber today is a combination of synthetic polymers and a small amount of natural rubber. Dy-Dee, on the other hand, is made of real rubber…natural rubber. Natural rubber is made from the sap of the Hevea brasiliensis tree. Unfortunately, natural materials (like the rubber derived from tree sap) will degrade over time. The good news for Dy-Dee collectors is that the process can be delayed.

There are three processes to be mindful of in considering the preservation of natural rubber artifacts: oxidation, biodeterioration and crystallization.

1. Oxidation is a chemical deterioration affected by temperature, low humidity, and light levels. The clue that oxidation is beginning is the formation of cracks in the rubber. To inhibit oxidation, temperature extremes must be avoided. The ideal temperature range to promote longevity of your dolls is 40-75 degrees Fahrenheit. Within the recommended temperature range, the humidity should be 50 percent. Because it is not practical to maintain humidity at a constant 50 percent, a range of 35-70 percent is acceptable. Ambient moisture below 35 percent promotes an unstable condition in natural rubber that can hasten oxidation. In addition to temperature and low humidity, oxidation and degradation of rubber is accelerated by light. Therefore, direct sunlight is most damaging to any doll. Ultraviolet filtering film for windows in your doll room is available from conservation companies. (See Resources on page 144.) The safest artificial light is fluorescent light from a source covered by a UV-filtering sleeve.

2. Biodeterioration is caused by an attack by microorganisms.

Peggy Montei worked on this doll over a long period of time first washing her and her clothing. Who would have believed that filthy dress could once again be made as white as the day it left the Effanbee Company? The sweater is now a lovely dusty-pink color. The body has been stuffed with pure cotton batting used for quilting. Peggy touched up the face and hair with oil paint, but only where absolutely necessary. Although this doll is still fragile, she is now lovely once again, and the cleaning process has hopefully slowed the rate of her deterioration.

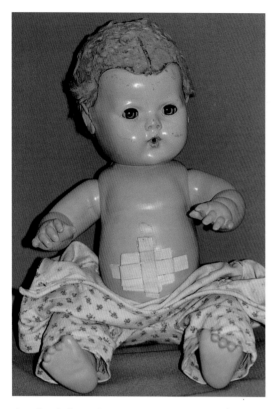

Another baby with an "owie" arrived at Peggy Montei's house with an unexplained bandage on her belly. (Perhaps the child mother of this baby had a new baby sibling at home when she was given this Dy-Dee.) Peggy noted the "skin" of the tummy was even slightly reddened around the edge of the bandage. This baby got a good sponge bath and had her hair washed several times, but Peggy chose to leave that thoughtfully placed little bandage on her tummy—a parting gift from her first child mother.

This process is initiated by moisture (ambient humidity) in excess of 70 percent. When the humidity drops below 70 percent, the destructive organisms will become dormant. But when the humidity rises again, the organisms will zealously continue their "meal."

3. Crystallization is a molecular restructuring that causes the material to lose its elasticity and dimension. Cracking and crumbling are evidence of crystallization. The loss of dimension in rubber is seen as a crack or shrinkage. Crystallization occurs naturally, but is hastened by contact with oils like petroleum products and greases. Some doll "doctors" unfortunately recommend the use of materials like Vaseline and/or cold cream (which is an emulsion of a fat in a water system) to "preserve" and "lubricate" rubber dolls. Admittedly, dolls treated with such materials do look better, initially. But the reality is that petroleum-based materials and greases promote deterioration and discoloration by crystallization over time. Another oil source that promotes deterioration is skin oil. Virtually all of the materials touted as protectants and rejuvenators for (natural) rubber leave a film that attracts airborne pollutants, such as dust, mold spore and other materials that can promote fungal attack under the right conditions. Ideally, white cotton gloves should be worn when handling rubber dolls if one wishes to preserve them. Skin oils also are a desirable nutrient substrate (read: delicious) for fungi. Air pollution also promotes the deterioration of natural rubber by crystallization. In a household, airborne microscopic fat particles from cooking or frying will also cause deterioration in rubber.

The life of a rubber doll can be prolonged with proper storage. Conversely, the life can be shortened by storage in an acid environment. Brown cardboard boxes, for example, are acidic.

In approaching preservation of a doll, you may want to think of a burnt cake: you cannot un-burn the cake no matter what you do. Likewise, a cracked rubber doll cannot be restored to like-new condition. But following a few rules will significantly slow deterioration:

1. Temperature range must remain between 40-75 degrees.

2. Relative humidity should remain close to the 35-70 percent range.

3. Contact with petroleum products, skin oils, waxes, silicones, acidic materials like brown cardboard boxes and any products called "protectant," "rejuvenator," "rubber aid," "dressing" or similar products must be avoided. Rubber dolls can be kept clean with a diluted liquid dish detergent or with diluted Formula 9-1-1. (See Resources on page 144.)

CHAPTER NINE

RECREATING THE DY-DEE BABY

I N AUGUST 2002 Robert Tonner, doll artist and president of the Tonner Doll Company, purchased the bankrupt Effanbee Doll Company, rescuing it from potential closure. A longtime doll collector, he was determined to revive the once-illustrious firm. He had long admired the portfolio of dolls created throughout Effanbee's ninety-three-year history and held in high regard the artists who created them—not only the prolific Bernard Lipfert, but also people like Dewees Cochran, who sculpted the American Children series of the 1940s and Sandra Bilotto, who sculpted the new Brenda Starr in the 1990s.

Since one of the famous faces of Effanbee during its most innovative years was Dy-Dee, it was a natural choice—as well as a challenge—to recreate a doll so well loved and distinctly made. Robert created the 2004 Dy-Dee using the most modern methods available to dollmakers today in combination with the lost-wax mold-making method, which is one of the oldest techniques known. The computer scanners and model makers used were all strictly "state of the art," and ensured that

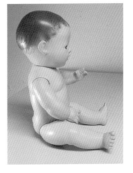

This original 11-inch Dy-Dee from the collection of Peggy Montei was used to create the new doll.

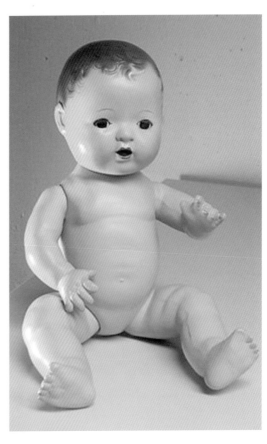

the proportions of the original Dy-Dee were not lost. The molds resulting from plating the tooling wax maintained all of the doll's fine detailing from the tip of Dy-Dee's molded hair to her curling toes. The Effanbee Doll Company's recreation process was documented in step-by-step photography, which is shared with readers on the following pages.

THE FIRST STEP in recreating Dy-Dee is to make a tooling wax prototype, from an original doll, from which molds for creating a new doll can be manufactured.

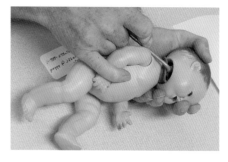

1. The disassembly of the original doll shows the mushroom joint that kept Dy-Dee dry when she was submerged in water.

2. The unique patented mushroom joint is removed for examination.

3. The view inside the head shows the blink-eye mechanism.

4. The disassembly of the arms and legs shows the special joints again.

5. This view of two versions of Dy-Dee shows a doll with molded ears and a doll with rubber ears removed.

6. Dy-Dee's head is scanned by computer for the upsizing of the mold.

7. Dy-Dee's legs are also scanned by the computer.

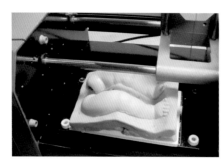

8. Plaster molds are made from the scanned pieces of the original doll; clay is used to build a side wall as each side of the mold is formed.

9. Tooling wax is poured into the plaster molds to create a prototype wax doll. (The wax is pink.)

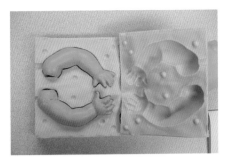

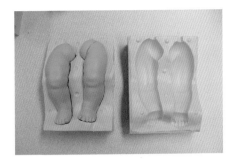

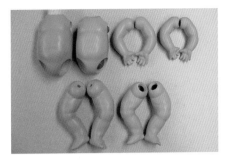

10. The rough waxes of the arms and legs, with the excess wax cleaned away, are shown in the plaster molds.

11. The original body parts, which are yellow, are shown with the pink tooling wax prototypes.

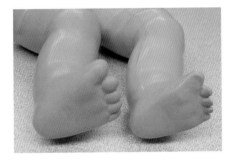

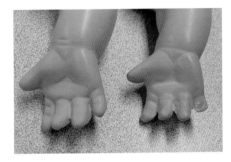

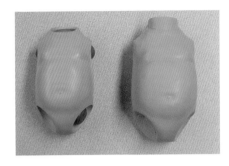

12. Close-up views of the pink tooling wax prototypes next to the original yellow body parts demonstrate the fidelity of the recreation.

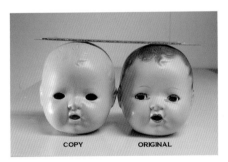

COPY   ORIGINAL

13. Compare the original head and the recreation in these front and side views. The tooling wax pieces are purposely larger than the originals to allow for shrinkage during manufacture.

14. The cleaned tooling wax prototype is assembled with the neck tube attached for electroplating.

15. Dy-Dee is officially named and dated in the tooling wax.

T HE NEXT STEP is to create a master mold from the tooling wax prototype. From this master mold, production molds are created. The doll parts are pulled from these molds, then assembled, painted and clothed.

1. The tooling wax pieces are cleaned before a master wax is created.

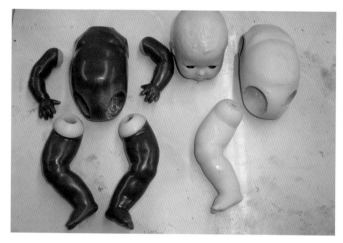

2. The dark-green master wax is developed from the pink tooling wax. It has engineered joints attached that are suitable for today's manufacturing process.

3. The master wax, with the appropriate joints attached, is now ready to be electroplated to produce the master mold. The wax will be "lost," or melted away, during the electroplating; this is known as the "lost wax" process.

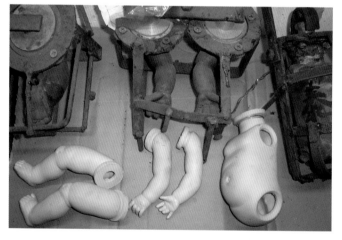

4. The master mold is used to produce multiple sets of master skins, which will be used to produce the production molds.

5. The master skin is submerged into an electroplating tank, where electronic current attracts metal to the surface. This process is duplicated to produce production molds, each made from a master skin pulled from the one master mold.

6. The heads are injection-molded, meaning that hard plastic is injected into the molds.

7. The molds are removed from the rotational-mold machine; note that the circular base rotates to coat the molds with liquid vinyl.

8. The bodies are rotationally molded; liquid vinyl is heated to produce a chemical change, which makes the liquid solidify. The warm, soft solidified vinyl is pulled through the small neck opening of the production mold.

9. Any rough edges are removed from the vinyl pieces by cleaning.

10. Dy-Dee's parts are assembled.

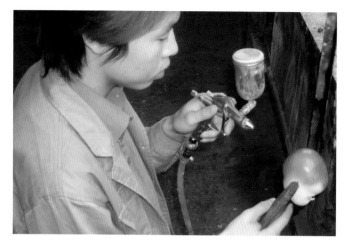

11. Dy-Dee's hair is spray painted onto her head.

12. A metal spray mask is used to paint the lips and eyebrows.

13. Certain details are hand painted.

14. The dolls' outfits are sewn by machine.

After being dressed, the new 11-inch Dy-Dee is ready to greet the world.

CHAPTER TEN

PATTERNS FOR AN 11-INCH DY-DEE LAYETTE

N O BOOK ON DY-DEE BABIES would be complete without a few patterns. Bradley Justice of Durham, North Carolina, who is well known as a maker of cloth dolls, teddy bears and fashionable doll clothing, has created a set of basic layette patterns for an 11-inch Dy-Dee. (With minor adjustments, they will also fit other 10 ½ and 11-inch baby dolls.) Bradley was given a solid foundation in the needle arts by his female relatives, and has training in pattern making and fashion design. He writes: *I remember the elaborate layettes Dy-Dee and the other baby dolls from that era had: lovely dresses, blankets, diapers, pillows, bottles and cuddly toys. Obviously, the little doll "mommies" had everything they needed to take care of their babies. I welcomed this opportunity to re-create a set of patterns to help today's doll mothers sew similar layettes for the dolls in their collections.*

Bradley's layette includes patterns and instructions for the following: diaper; bib; romper; booties; panties; footed pajamas; nightgown; dress (short and christening), slip; bonnet, sacque; and blanket. The patterns are made to fit an 11-inch Dy-Dee doll and include a ⅛-inch seam allowance. As always when sewing, it is best to make the pattern in muslin or paper towel and fit it on your doll before cutting into your fabric.

All of the garments in the layette were created using a sewing machine, but they can easily be stitched by hand. Simple purchased embellishments have been used for these examples. If you enjoy doing hand-embroidery, however, that is entirely appropriate for layette clothing. You may substitute appropriately sized ribbon for the bias tape, if you want a slightly fancier look.

Short dress and bonnet

Christening dress and blanket

DRESS *(patterns: pp. 134-135)*
Pattern Pieces: Bodice and Sleeve

For the bodice, cut 2 pieces, one for the bodice and one for lining. Stitch as indicated by broken lines on the pattern. Clip curves, turn and press. Sew the side seams.

For the skirt, cut a piece of fabric 5 inches long by 23 inches wide (the 23-inch width is gathered to fit the waist). This includes a one-inch hem. Using two rows of gathering stitches, gather skirt to fit waist. Sew skirt to bottom edge of bodice. Sew back seam 4 inches up from hem. Turn under 1/8 inch on bottom edge and stitch. Turn up hem 1/2 inch. The finished length of the skirt should be about 4 inches. Use three buttons and thread loops, or snaps, to close the upper back.

If you want to add puffed sleeves to this dress, omit sewing around the armhole "eyes." To make the sleeves, cut two. Hem the lower edge of the sleeve. If desired, attach slightly gathered lace to edge. Gather the top of the sleeve between the two points indicated to fit the armhole opening. Stitch the sleeve to the armhole before stitching the side seam. Stitch the side seam. Then continue and attach skirt as instructed above.

To turn the dress pattern into a christening gown, cut the skirt fabric 12 inches long by 23 inches wide and follow the above instructions.

BLANKET
No pattern piece required

A blanket for an 11-inch doll can be plain or fancy; whichever you choose it is simple to stitch. Cut a piece of cotton flannel 19 inches square. Select a bias tape in a contrasting color that coordinates with other layette items. By machine or by hand, stitch the tape to blanket. After stitching, decorate the bias tape with an embroidery stitch of your choice or a simple straight stitch using two strands of embroidery floss. If you want to make a dressier blanket, use silk or satin ribbon to edge your blanket.

You may also cut two squares of fabric, each 19 inches by 19 inches.

With the right sides together, stitch, leaving a small opening on one side for turning. Clip the corners, turn and press. You may leave it plain or embellish with simple appliqué or embroidery.

For a more elaborate blanket, use a ruffled lace edge, or gathered eyelet on the edge. You may also use lace or eyelet "beading" through which you may run a co-ordinating ribbon, across one corner of the blanket.

When Dy-Dee was introduced, there was a marvelous fabric for baby layettes called *eiderdown*. We do not have that fabric today, but you may want to make a nice cozy blanket from the new polar fleeces that are available in various weights, colors, and designs. They do not ravel, so you can finish your edge with a pretty blanket stitch, by machine or by hand. You may also clip the edge to form a fringe, instead.

DIAPER *(pattern: p. 135)*

There are several ways to create a diaper. Two pieces of cotton flannel, or diaper flannel, can be cut from the pattern piece. With the right sides together, stitch all around the diaper, leaving a small opening on the center back for turning. Close the opening with a blind stitch. You may also trace the pattern onto cotton flannel. Finish the edge with satin stitching on the sewing machine before cutting out the diaper. The simplest diaper is made by tracing the pattern onto the flannel and cutting it out with pinking shears. Secure the diaper with one safety pin.

The original Dy-Dee had these formed diapers, but also had rectangular diapers cut of Birdseye fabric, stitched with a narrow little hem. If you prefer the rectangular-style diaper, you will need a piece of Birdseye fabric that is 6 inches wide by 8 inches long. Turn the edge under ¼ inch on all four sides, and stitch with contrasting thread or two strands of embroidery floss. Secure the diaper with two pins.

FOOTED PAJAMAS

(pattern: p. 136)

Placing the pattern edge on the fold of the fabric as indicated on the pattern, cut one piece for the front. Using pattern, cut two pieces for the back. Use flannel, cotton seersucker or a knit fabric. With the right sides together, sew each back to the front at the shoulder seams. Attach the bias tape to the lower edge of each sleeve. Sew the lower back together, leaving 4 inches open

Footed pajamas

from the neckline down. Edge the back opening with bias tape. Leaving a 5-inch tail to form one side of the tie, edge the neck opening with bias tape, ending with another 5-inch tail. On the wrong side of the fabric, trace a line for the elastic on lower leg. Stretch and stitch the elastic to this line, forming a little foot. Sew the back and front together under each arm.

BOOTIES *(pattern: p. 136)*

Cut four from a knit fabric. Using a zig-zag stitch on the sewing machine, sew across the straight top edge of the booty, stretching lightly as you sew. With the right sides together, sew around the outer edge of the booty. Turn and embellish with a pompom on the toe. You may also use a double-knit fabric, or the undamaged portion

of an old fine-gauge sweater. If you use a sweater knit, stitch around each piece before beginning to make the booties as described.

SLIP *(pattern: p. 137)*

Cut two (one front and one front facing). Cut two backs and two back facings. Stitch a tiny hem in the lower edge of the lining. With the right sides together, sew the side seams on the slip. With the right sides together, sew the side seams on the facing. With right sides together, sew facing to slip around the armholes, over the shoulders, and around the neck. Clip curves, turn and press. This will give your little slip a nicely finished top-edge. Attach the buttons and make button loops to secure the slip over the shoulders. Or you may attach ribbons and simply tie the slip at the shoulders. To use the slip with the christening gown, use enough fabric to match the length of the dress pattern above.

ROMPER *(pattern: p. 138)*

Cut the single pattern piece. Edge the armhole with bias tape. Sew the shoulder seams. Using bias tape, start at point A on the pattern, and work towards the neck edge. Edge the back waistline of the romper with bias tape, leaving a 6-inch piece as you begin, and

Romper (front and back) and booties

another 6-inch piece as you finish on the other side, creating a "sash" to tie in front and secure the romper. Contrasting bias tape is recommended as trim.

BONNET *(pattern: p. 139)*

Cut two: one piece of fabric for the outer side of bonnet and one contrasting piece for the lining. Match the points as marked on the pattern and sew seams from A to B. With right sides together, begin sewing at point A and around, leaving the seam open at the lower back edge for turning. Clip curves, turn and press. Sew ribbon, or bias made from the same fabric or commercial bias tape in a straight line, leaving a 7-inch tail on either side to tie under the doll's chin. Embellish with embroidery or appliqué. By using the contrasting lining, you have created a reversible bonnet.

PANTIES *(pattern: p. 140)*

Cut two pieces. With the right sides together, sew the front seam. Hem the leg openings. Stitch the elastic $1/4$ inch from the hem, stretching as you sew. Turn down the waist-line and stitch elastic, stretching as you sew. Sew the back seam and then sew the crotch seam.

BIB *(pattern: p. 141)*

Cut two pieces of flannel or, if you want the bib to match a particular outfit, cut one piece of flannel and one of the fabric used for the outfit. With the right sides together, stitch around the bib, leaving a small opening at the center front neckline for turning. Clip curves, turn and press. Then add a 14-inch piece of bias tape or silk ribbon to enclose the top of bib and extend it to create ties for securing the bib on the doll. Embellish with embroidery or a small rosette.

NIGHTGOWN

(pattern: pp. 140-141)

Cut two on fold, then split one piece along the dotted line to form back opening. With right sides together, stitch the shoulders. Fold under sleeve end and hem, or bind with contrasting ribbon or bias tape. Turn under the raw edges of the back opening; hem. Enclose the neck edge with ribbon or bias tape. Add a 6-inch ribbon to each side of the back neck opening to tie neckline. Stitch the underarm seam. Turn up the hem and sew it in place. Be sure the hem is wide enough to form a casing through which you can slide a ribbon or twill tape to

Nightgown

gather the lower edge of the nightgown. You may also simply hem the bottom of the nightgown and embellish with gathered cotton lace.

SACQUE *(at right)*

Sacque and panties

Lay the sacque pattern piece along the fold of your fabric and cut one. Cut from the neckline to the end of the piece on one side to form the two front pieces. Turn under a narrow hem along the front pieces and stitch. Turn under the lower edge of the seams on the sleeves and hem, or edge with bias tape. Bind neck with bias tape. Sew the side and underarm seams. Clip curves and press. Then turn under narrow hem on the lower edge of the sacque and stitch. Cut two pieces of ribbon 6 inches long each to form tie, or make narrow ties to coordinate to the neck binding.

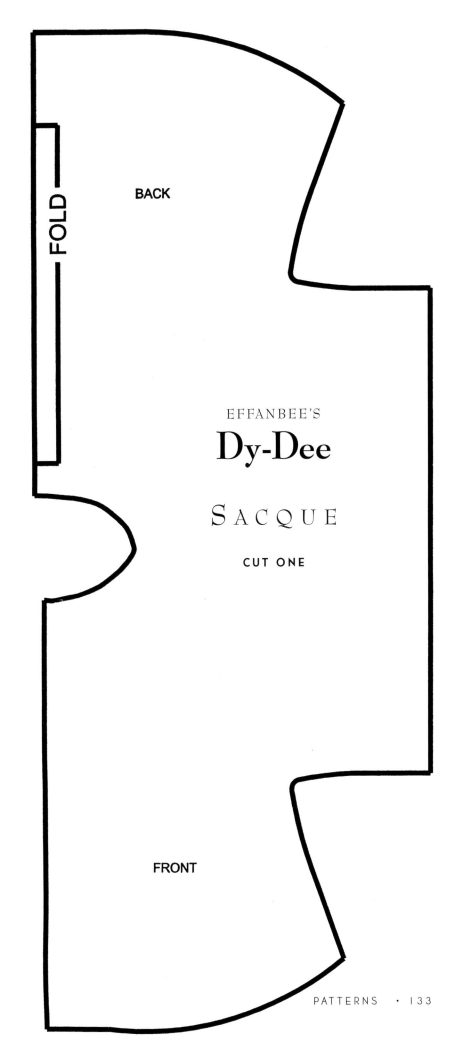

FOLD

BACK

EFFANBEE'S
Dy-Dee

SACQUE

CUT ONE

FRONT

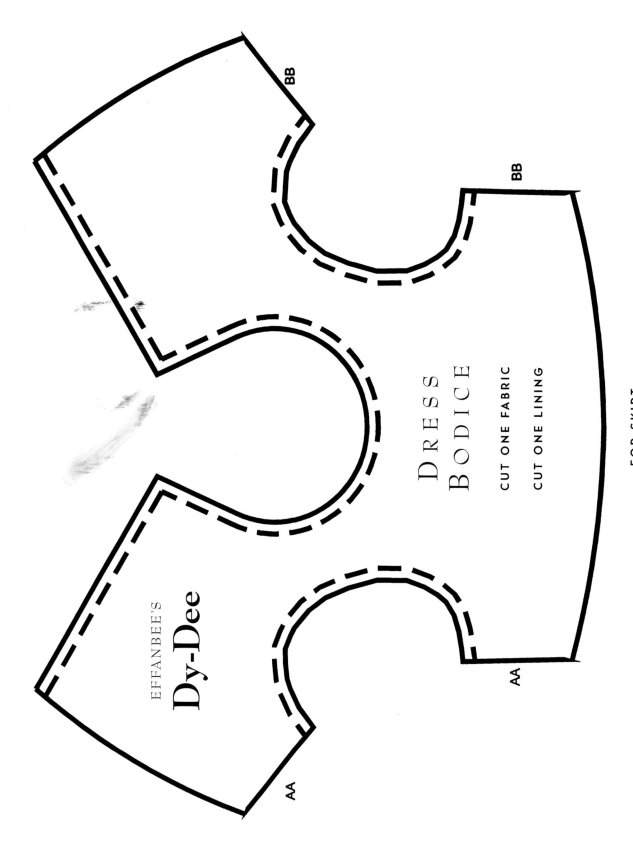

EFFANBEE'S
Dy-Dee

DRESS
BODICE

CUT ONE FABRIC

CUT ONE LINING

BB

BB

AA

AA

FOR SKIRT
CUT PIECE OF FABRIC
5'' WIDE X 23'' LONG (1'' HEM)

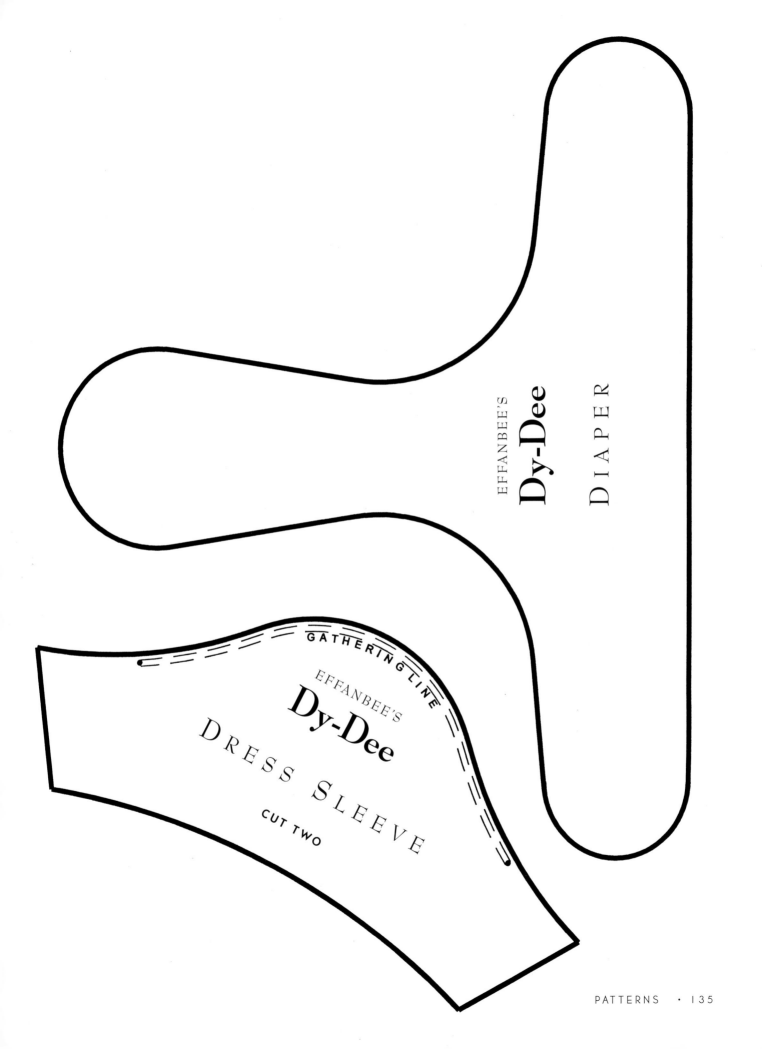

EFFANBEE'S
Dy-Dee
DIAPER

GATHERING LINE

EFFANBEE'S
Dy-Dee
DRESS SLEEVE
CUT TWO

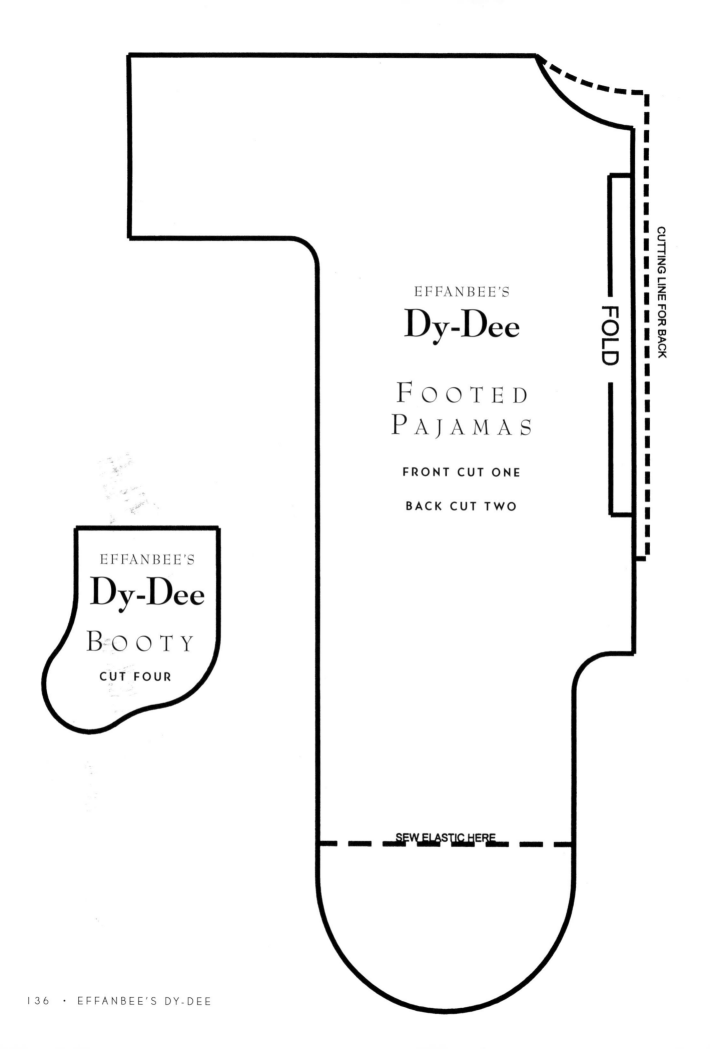

EFFANBEE'S
Dy-Dee

FOOTED PAJAMAS

FRONT CUT ONE

BACK CUT TWO

FOLD

CUTTING LINE FOR BACK

SEW ELASTIC HERE

EFFANBEE'S
Dy-Dee

BOOTY

CUT FOUR

EFFANBEE'S **Dy-Dee**

S L I P
F R O N T

CUT ONE

CUT HERE FOR FACING

EFFANBEE'S **Dy-Dee**

S L I P
B A C K

CUT TWO

CUT HERE FOR FACING

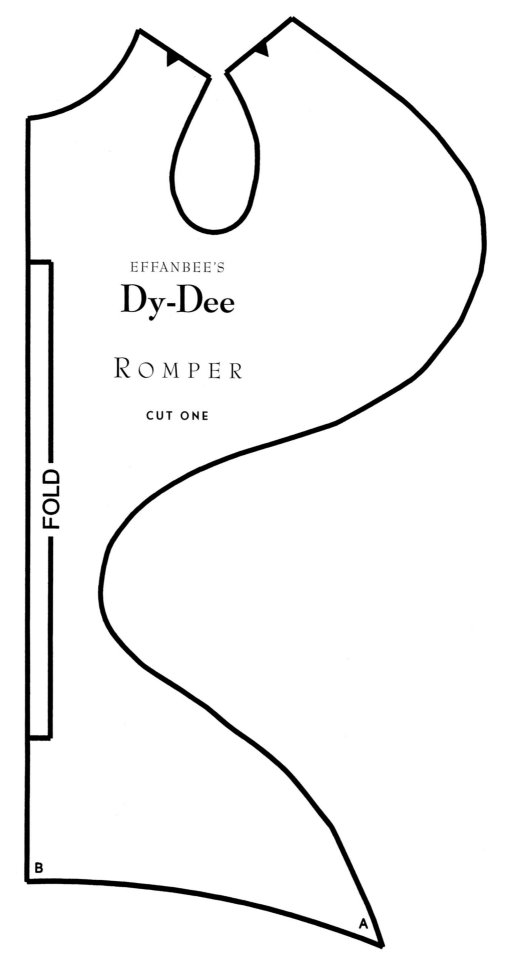

EFFANBEE'S
Dy-Dee

ROMPER

CUT ONE

FOLD

B

A

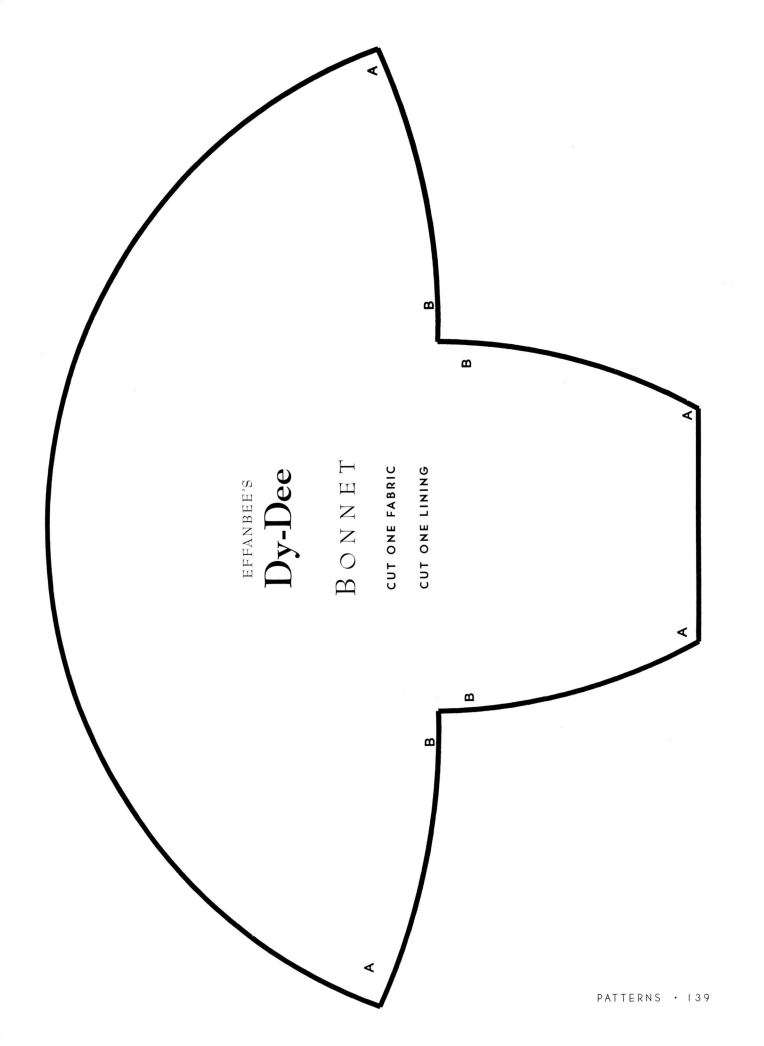

EFFANBEE'S
Dy-Dee
BONNET

CUT ONE FABRIC

CUT ONE LINING

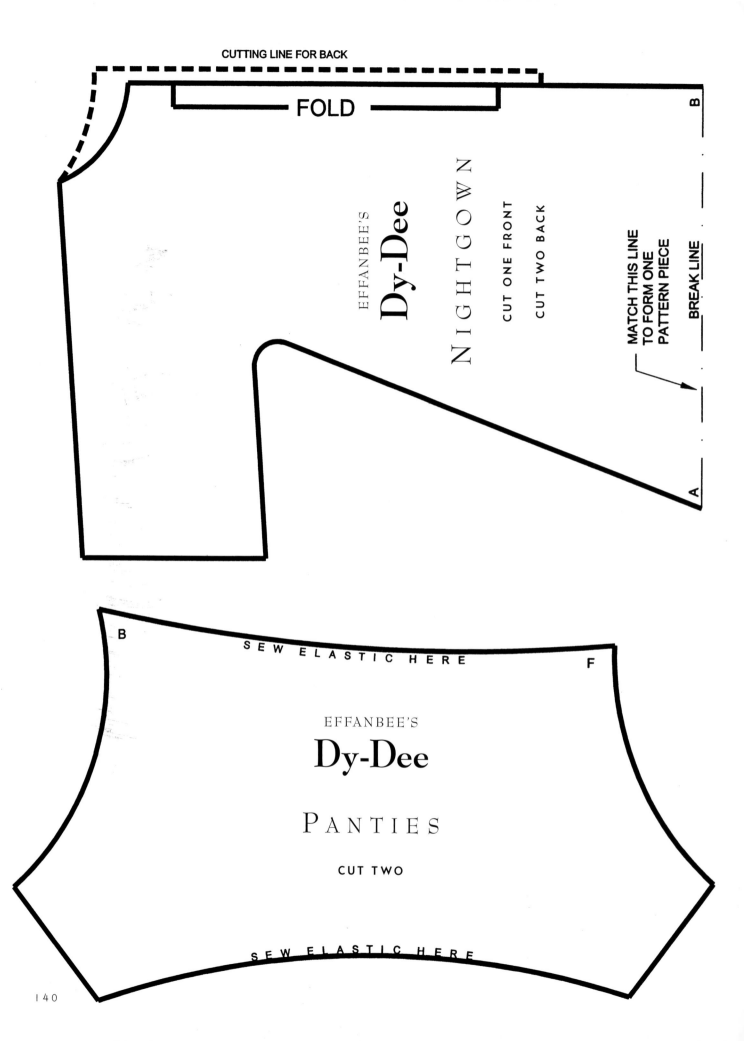

CUTTING LINE FOR BACK

FOLD

B

EFFANBEE'S **Dy-Dee** NIGHTGOWN

CUT ONE FRONT

CUT TWO BACK

MATCH THIS LINE TO FORM ONE PATTERN PIECE

BREAK LINE

A

B   SEW ELASTIC HERE   F

EFFANBEE'S

Dy-Dee

PANTIES

CUT TWO

SEW ELASTIC HERE

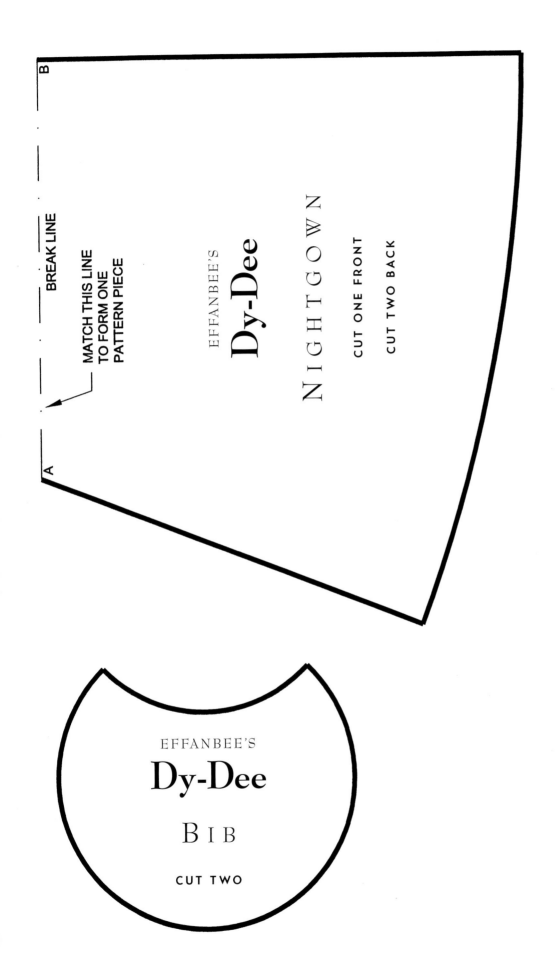

B

BREAK LINE

MATCH THIS LINE
TO FORM ONE
PATTERN PIECE

EFFANBEE'S
Dy-Dee

NIGHTGOWN

CUT ONE FRONT

CUT TWO BACK

A

EFFANBEE'S
Dy-Dee

BIB

CUT TWO

BIBLIOGRAPHY

Axe, John. *Effanbee: A Collector's Encyclopedia 1949-1983*. Cumberland, MD: Hobby House Press, 1983.

Axe, John and, Schoonmaker, Patricia. *Effanbee: 75 Years of Dolls That Touch Your Heart*. Cumberland, MD: Hobby House Press, 1985.

Burdick, Loraine. "Dy-dee Baby Paper Doll," *Doll Reader*, April 1990, pp. 178-182.

_____. "Data on Dy-dee," *Celebrity Doll Journal*, Year 29, No. 4, August 1995, pp. 1-16.

Coleman, Dorothy S., Elizabeth A., & Evelyn J. *The Collector's Encyclopedia of Dolls, Vol. I*. New York, NY: Crown Publishing, 1968.

_____. *The Collector's Encyclopedia of Dolls, Vol. II*. New York, NY: Crown Publishing, 1986.

_____. *The Collector's Book of Doll Clothes*. New York, NY: Crown Publishing, 1975.

Formanek-Brunell, Miriam. *Made to Play House: Dolls and the Commercialization of American Girlhood, 1830-1939*. New Haven, CT: Yale University Press, 1993.

Grun, Bernard. *The Timetables of History*. New York, NY: Simon & Schuster, 1972.

Hill, Nicholas J. *The Definitive Book on the Care and Preservation of Vinyl Dolls and Action Figures*. Scarborough, ME: Twin Pines Press, 2000.

Holden, Queen. *Dy-dee Baby Doll Cutout Book*. New York, NY: Whitman, 1938.

Holderbaum, Linda Poirier. "Dolls of the Post-WW II Era," *Doll Reader*, August-September 1987, pp. 154-155.

Jensen, Don. "Elusive Aunt Patsy," *Patsy & Friends*, No. 79, September-October 2000, pp. 16-17.

Johnson, JoAnn. "Repairing Dy-dee Louise: Bringing Dy-dee Louise back to life with these repair tips," *International Doll World*, July-August 1991, pp. 24-26.

Johnson, JoAnn. "Caring for and Restoring Rubber Dolls," *International Doll World*, July-August 1991, pp. 22-23.

Martin, Martha M. "Baby Doll: A Case of Mistaken

Identity," *Doll Reader*, November 1995, p. 72.

Matthews, Glenna. *Just A Housewife: The Rise and Fall of Domesticity in America*, New York, NY: Oxford University Press, 1987.

Moyer, Patsy. *Modern Collectible Dolls, Vol.III*. Paducah, KY: Collector Books, 1999

Schoonmaker, Patricia N. *Effanbee Dolls: The Formative Years, 1910-1929*. Cumberland, MD: Hobby House Press, 1984.

_____. *Patsy Doll Family Encyclopedia, Vol. II*. Cumberland, MD: Hobby House Press, 1998.

Smith, Patricia R.. *Effanbee: Dolls that Touch Your Heart*. Paducah, KY: Collector Books, 1983.

Stuecher, Mary Rickert. "Drink & Wet Babies: Betsy Wetsy and Tiny Tears," *Doll Reader*, February-March 1984, pp. 60-67.

Stuecher, Mary Rickert. "Drink & Wet Babies: The Dy-dee Doll," Part 1, *Doll Reader*, December 1983-January 1984, pp.90-96.

Twigg, Bettyanne Bethea. "Collecting, Preserving and Displaying Rubber Dolls," *Doll Reader*, October 1985, pp. 82-91.

Zillner, Dian. *Dolls & Accessories of the 1930s and 1940s*. Atglen, PA: Schiffer Publishing, 2002.

Zillner, Dian. "Early Drink & Wet Dolls," *Doll Reader*, May 1990, pp. 212-219.

"Dolls—Made in America," *Fortune* magazine, December 1936, pp. 103-200.

"750,000 Dy-dee Dolls Gratify the Maternal Instinct of Modern Youngsters," *Life* magazine, November 22, 1937, pp. 55-58.

PATSY & FRIENDS NEWSLETTER

Vol. 2, No. 1, 1989, pp. 18-19.
Vol. 4, No. 25, 1991, pp. 18, 21, 28-29.
Vol. 6, No. 35, 1993, pp. 5, 7, 11, 13-16, 20-21, 24-29.
Vol. 6, No. 36, 1993, pp. 10,14-15, 28.

EFFANBEE PUBLICATIONS

My Doll's Magazine, Fleischaker & Baum, 1931.
Aunt Patsy Tells A Story, Fleischaker & Baum, 1938.
What Every Doll Mother Should Know, Fleischaker & Baum.
How to Select the Proper Doll to Suit Your Child's Age, (for adults) Fleischaker & Baum.
How to Play With a Doll, Fleischaker & Baum.

THE PATSYTOWN NEWS, FLEISCHAKER & BAUM, 1934-1938.

Vol. 1, No. 2, "Extra! New Dy-dee Baby Arrives!" 1934.
Vol. 1, No. 3, "Dy-dee Captures Millions of Hearts," 1934.
Vol. 2, No. 1, "Dy-dee Now America's Most Popular Doll," 1935.
Vol. 2, No. 2, "Extra—Dy-dee Now Has Baby Sister," 1935.
Vol. 3, No. 1, "I Take Dy-dee to the Seashore," 1936.
Vol. 3, No. 2, "Dy-dee is the Doll I Want!" 1936.
Vol. 4, No. 1, "Dy-dee Is the Doll I Want, Doll Mothers Tell Aunt Patsy," 1937.
Vol. 4, No. 2, "Charlie McCarthy Visits Patsytown... Admits He Thought Babies were a Bother Until He Visited the Dy-dee Nursery," 1937.
Vol. 5, No. 1, "Dy-dee's Clothes Are Talk of Patsytown, 1938.

RESOURCES & CONTRIBUTORS

The following are good sources for conservation materials to help preserve your Dy-Dee dolls.

Conservation Emporium
100 Standing Rock Circle
Reno, NV 89511
Telephone: 775-852-0404
www.consemp.com

Light Impressions
P.O. Box 22708
Rochester, NY 14692-2708
Telephone: 800-828-6216
www.lightimpressionsdirect.com

Gaylord Brothers
P.O. Box 22708
Syracuse, NY 13221-4901
Telephone: 800-634-6307
www.gaylord.com

University Products
P.O. Box 101
Holyoke, MA 01041-0101
Telephone: 800-628-1912
www.universityproducts.com

The author would like to extend her appreciation to all those who contributed to this book.

Jill Sander
Sue Cummings
Jan Mackenize
Marsha Hayek
Vickie Townsend
Linda Mangold
Loraine Burdick
Kate Gillen
Jean Sullivan
Jean…gardenias@nyc.rr.com

John Axe
Michelle Hall
Val Hays
Ida…..idasdolls@yahoo.com
Nick & Barbara Hill
Ellen...ellenk@exploratorium.edu
Sharon Smith
Sue Cummings
Pam Nowain
Joan Pursley

Leah Kalin
Peggy Major
Barbara Starkey
Patsy Moyer
Shirley McCoy
Linda Ludwig
Patricia Schoonmaker
Bradley Justice
Betsy Spear
Karen Friesner

PHOTOGRAPHERS

Jack Hilliker
James Brownell
Peggy Montei

Photos on pages 2, 6, 8, 23, 34, 52, 80, 94, 108: Robert M. Talbot

ADDITIONAL CAPTIONS

Page 2: Dy-Dee from Mold 2 wears an Effanbee dotted-Swiss dress with pink embroidery and a portrait bonnet with wide organdy ruffle. She holds her Effanbee layette nursing bottle with its original pink plastic nipple-protector cap still in place.

Page 6: Dy-Dee from Mold 3 wears her Effanbee cotton flannel robe and blue-flowered flannel pajamas.

A book is never the product of one person's efforts. I wish to acknowledge the support, encouragement and talent of my editor, Krystyna Goddu, and the skilled layout design by Arlene Lappen. Their talents and foresight, as well as Thomas Farrell's guidance, have made this beautiful book a reality. —*Barbara Craig Hilliker*